D1414961

Geometry

Chad Troutwine · Markus Moberg · Chris Kane · Mark Glenn · Brian Galvin

Co-Founders	Chad Troutwine
	Markus Moberg
Managing Editor	Mark Glenn
Director of Academic Programs	Brian Galvin
Interior Design	Lisa Johnson
	Miriam Lubow
Cover Design	Nick Mason
	Mike Miller
Contributing Editors	Jim Stekelberg
	Joseph Dise
	Jason Sun
	Jeff Lev
Contributing Writers	Laura Cook
	Jim Stekelberg

A successful educational program is only as good as the people who teach it, and Veritas Prep is fortunate to have many of the world's finest GMAT instructors on its team.

Not only does that team know how to teach a strong curriculum, but it also knows how to help create one. This lesson book would not be possible without the hundreds of suggestions we have received from our talented faculty all across the world — from Seattle, Detroit, and Miami to London, Singapore, and Dubai. Their passion for excellence helped give birth to a new curriculum that is far better than what we could have created on our own.

Our students also deserve a very special thanks. Thousands of them have provided us with something priceless: enthusiastic feedback that has guided us in creating the most comprehensive GMAT preparation course available on the market today.

We therefore dedicate this revised lesson book to all Veritas Prep instructors and students who have tackled the GMAT and given us their valuable input along the way.

Table of Contents

Lesson 6 Introduction

The branch of mathematics known as Geometry is enormous and wide-ranging. Fortunately, there is only a limited number of Geometry topics tested on the GMAT. Your top-scoring Veritas Prep instructor, drawing on our tried-and-true curriculum, will teach you to see through the test makers' distractions to those topics for which you are responsible. Once you have fully absorbed this lesson, you will be able to break down even the most lengthy and complex Geometry problem into a series of small, straightforward tasks.

Geometry

Each section in this lesson will contain a review of the basic properties relating to certain figures followed by the application of more difficult concepts with questions. While geometry problems may be some of the most complicated of all the Data Sufficiency and Problem Solving problems, the types of geometry problems you may encounter on the GMAT are restricted in scope. Today geometry makes up approximately 10-15% of the quantitative portion of the GMAT (4 - 6 questions).

Lines and Angles

Lines and angles are the fundamental building blocks of geometry. Although the rules relating to lines and angles are relatively simple, it is important to be comfortable with them.

Try the following problem, which relies on principles covered in the Math Essentials Lesson (as well as some algebra):

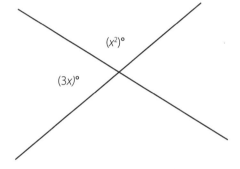

<u>Note:</u> Figure not drawn to scale.

1. In the figure above, what is the value of x?

(A)   9

(B)   12

(C)   15

(D)   18

(E)   36

GMAT Insider: Be very careful when using figures to answer geometry questions. According to the test maker, figures and diagrams on Problem Solving questions are "drawn as accurately as possible" UNLESS they are labeled "NOT DRAWN TO SCALE." On Data Sufficiency questions, and any questions with figures labeled "NOT DRAWN TO SCALE," figures are often intentionally manipulated to sucker you into making false assumptions. Do not use such figures to make any guesses about lengths, angle measures, etc.

Facts & Formulas: Two intersecting lines form four angles with two pairs of angles being identical on opposite sides of the intersection. The sum of two angles on one side of a line is always 180°.

Sometimes the easiest geometry rules are the key to solving complex geometry problems. Most GMAT geometry problems require the application of numerous rules to solve them, so students should train themselves to apply all potential rules to a particular problem.

Triangles

Triangles are the most important shape tested on the GMAT. Make sure that you have the basic triangle formulas down cold. The key to solving dificult geometry problems often lies in finding creative ways to apply these triangle formulas. Look for triangles even in problems that seem to be about circles, trapezoids, etc.

Facts & Formulas: The perimeter of a triangle is the sum of the lengths of its sides.

$P = a + b + c.$

The area of a triangle is its base multiplied by its height divided by two.

$A = \dfrac{b \cdot h}{2}$

Important Triangle Concepts:

I.) Right Triangles

A **right** angle triangle (one angle equals 90°) allows us to calculate the length of one side when we know the length of two other sides, by using $a^2 + b^2 = c^2$.

Right triangles are an integral part of geometry on the GMAT and must be mastered by students. In the online lesson, you should have refreshed your use of basic Pythagorean theory. In this section we will look at some of the common right triangles and how they are tested.

Right Triangles with Certain Sides

While students must be prepared to deal with any combination of sides with right triangles, there are a couple specific right triangles with whole number sides that are frequently used on the GMAT. The right triangles below, with sides **3, 4, 5**, and **5, 12, 13**, are those commonly used triangles. Note that the sides of these triangles may be any multiple of the side given in these example (e.g. 6, 8, 10 or 2.5, 6, 6.5, etc.)

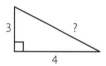

$a = 3$
$b = 4$
Find c.

Because one angle is 90° we can use the Pythagorean Theorem: $a^2 + b^2 = c^2$

Substitute the variables with their known values:
$3^2 + 4^2 = c^2 \rightarrow 9 + 16 = c^2 \rightarrow 25 = c^2 \rightarrow c = 5$

> *GMAT Insider:* It is essential that you recognize these common right triangles so that you do not have to waste valuable time using the Pythagorean Theorem to determine the third side. Also, you still need to know two sides in these triangles to determine the third side. In other words, knowing that one side of a right triangle is 3 is not enough to determine that the other two are 4 and 5.

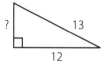

$b = 12$
$c = 13$
Find a.

Because one angle is 90° we can use the Pythagorean Theorem:
$a^2 + b^2 = c^2$

Substitute the variables with their known values:
$a^2 + 12^2 = 13^2 \rightarrow a^2 + 144 = 169 \rightarrow a^2 = 169 - 144 \rightarrow a^2 = 25 \rightarrow a = 5$

Right Triangles with Certain Angles

Two other very common right triangles are ones with the angles 30, 60, 90 and 45, 45, 90. These are unique because in these triangles you only need to know one side to determine the other two sides because of unique proportions that exist.

30-60-90 Triangles

A triangle with the angles 30, 60 and 90, always has sides with lengths of the proportions 1, $\sqrt{3}$, and 2. Note that $2x$ is the longest side, so $2x$ belongs on the hypotenuse. Similarly, x is the shortest side and belongs on the side opposite the 30° angle. $\sqrt{3}x$, as the length of the medium side, belongs opposite of the 60° angle.

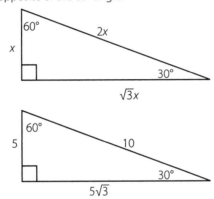

Example: In the following two triangles give the value of side y.

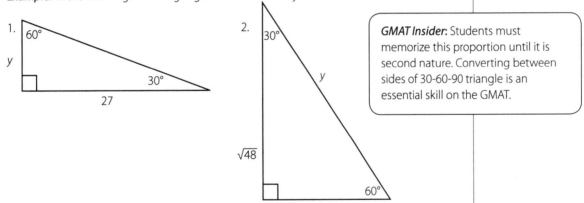

> **GMAT Insider:** Students must memorize this proportion until it is second nature. Converting between sides of 30-60-90 triangle is an essential skill on the GMAT.

In the first triangle we must divide the side opposing 60° by $\sqrt{3}$ to determine the short side (the side opposing 30º). After this division and removing the root from the denominator we see that $y = 9\sqrt{3}$.

In the second triangle, we must use the same procedure to determine the short side so we divide $\sqrt{48}$ by $\sqrt{3}$ and find that the short side is 4. We must then double that to determine the hypotenuse so, $y = 8$.

45-45-90 Triangles (AKA Right Isosceles Triangles)

A triangle with the angles 45, 45 and 90, always has sides with lengths of the proportions 1, 1, and $\sqrt{2}$:

Example: In the following triangle, what is the value of side y?

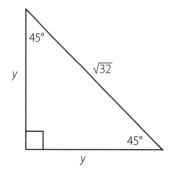

To determine the short sides of a 45-45-90 triangle, we must divide the hypotenuse by $\sqrt{2}$.

$\frac{\sqrt{32}}{\sqrt{2}} = \sqrt{\frac{32}{2}} = \sqrt{16} = 4$. Therefore $y = 4$ in this example.

Note

A 45-45-90 triangle is simply one half of a square. Therefore when determining the diagonal of a square use the relationship you have learned with the 45-45-90 triangle.

II.) Isosceles Triangles

An **isosceles** triangle has at least two sides and two angles that are the same.

When an altitude is drawn in an isosceles triangle from the unequal side, it always creates two equal triangles. In other words, the altitude splits the base and the angle evenly when drawn from the unequal side. In the following diagram, isosceles triangle ABC is split by an altitude drawn from the vertex at point B to the point D on unequal side AC. Because of this rule we know that AD=DC, angle ABD = angle DBC and triangle ABD is congruent (equal) to triangle DBC.

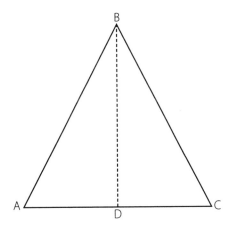

Now try the following problem:

2.   In an isosceles triangle DEF, what is the measure of angle EDF?

   (1)   Angle DEF is 96 degrees.

   (2)   Angle DFE is 42 degrees.

(A)   Statement (1) ALONE is sufficient, but statement (2) alone is not sufficient.

(B)   Statement (2) ALONE is sufficient, but statement (1) alone is not sufficient.

(C)   BOTH statements TOGETHER are sufficient, but NEITHER statement ALONE

        is sufficient.

(D)   EACH statement ALONE is sufficient.

(E)   Statements (1) and (2) TOGETHER are NOT sufficient.

III.) Equilateral Triangles

In an **equilateral** triangle, all sides are of equal length and all angles are 60°.

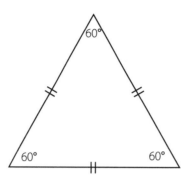

Since an isosceles triangle is one with **at least** two sides and two angles equal, every equilateral triangle is also an isosceles triangle. Equilateral triangles are very common on the GMAT and possess several important properties that students need to memorize.

When you draw in the height of an equilateral triangle, two 30-60-90 triangles are formed. Using the 30-60-90 ratios we just learned, you can deduce that the height of an equilateral triangle will always be $\frac{\sqrt{3}}{2}$ times the side of the triangle. As with all triangles, the area of an equilateral triangle is $\frac{1}{2}$ Base x Height.

Facts & Formulas: The area of an equilateral triangle $= \frac{(s^2\sqrt{3})}{4}$ where s is the side of the equilateral triangle. It is not required to memorize this formula – you can always derive the answer using 30-60-90 ratios – but some students have found that memorization saves precious time on the test.

GMAT Insider: If you are working with an equilateral triangle, any extra piece of information is enough to determine everything about that triangle. For instance, if you know the perimeter of an equilateral triangle than you can determine the area. If you know the area, then you can always find the sides.

3.   If an equilateral triangle has an area of $\sqrt{243}$, then what is the perimeter of that triangle?

(A)   6

(B)   12

(C)   18

(D)   27

(E)   81

IV.) Assorted Properties of Triangles

There are several other important qualities of triangles that are commonly tested on the GMAT. Let's examine the first with a real GMAT question that highlights how important it is to know even the most obscure geometry rules:

4.   If 7 and 10 are the lengths of two sides of a triangular region, which of the following can be the length of the third side?

(I.) 2
(II.) 8
(III.) 17

(A)   II only

(B)   III only

(C)   I and II only

(D)   II and III only

(E)   I, II, and III

Facts & Formulas: *Third Side Rule*
The third side of a triangle is always greater than the difference of the other two sides and less than the sum of the other 2 sides. This applies to every side of a triangle. In other words, you can arbitrarily pick any one side to be the "third side" and then that side must be greater than the difference of the other 2 and less than the sum of those two.

Because of the third side rule, it is clear in this problem that the third side x must meet these conditions: $3 < x < 17$. The only answer given that meets these conditions is 8 so the answer is II only (A).

Triangles with Supplementary Angles (Adding up to 180°)

Recognizing triangles with supplementary angles is an important skill for many difficult GMAT problems. In the following diagram consider the properties of the angles a, b, c, and d. We know that $c + d = 180$ and we know that $c + (a + b) = 180$. Therefore, using basic algebra it is always true that $d = a + b$.

Facts & Formulas: *Exterior Angles*
Whenever a supplementary angle is drawn off of an interior angle of a triangle as in the preceding diagram, it will always equal the sum of the other two interior angles of the triangle. Recognizing this quickly will give you an advantage on many difficult geometry problems.

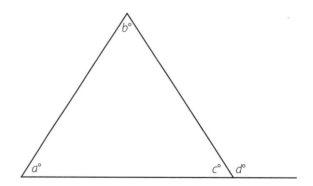

Similar Triangles

Similar triangles are triangles in which all the angles of the two triangles are the same. In similar triangles, the proportion of corresponding sides and heights is constant. Consider the following diagram that shows two similar triangles and their corresponding sides:

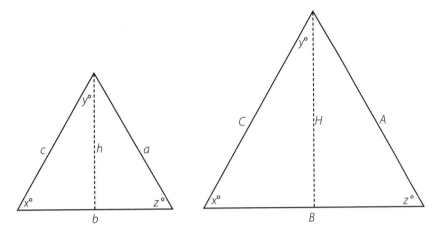

Because the angles are the same in each triangle, we know that the ratio of corresponding sides and heights is constant in the two triangles. In other words:

$$\frac{a}{A} = \frac{b}{B} = \frac{c}{C} = \frac{h}{H}$$

There are three standard ways to identify that triangles are similar.

AAA (Angle Angle Angle): If the angle measures in one triangle match the angle measures in the other triangle, then the triangles are similar. Note, you actually only need to match two sets of angles.

SSS (Side Side Side): If there is a constant ratio of corresponding sides for two triangles, then the triangles are similar. That is, if $\frac{a}{A} = \frac{b}{B} = \frac{c}{C}$, then the triangles are similar.

SAS (Side Angle Side): If there is a constant ratio of corresponding sides for 2 sets of sides AND if the angle between those two sides is the same in the first triangle as it is in the second triangle, then the triangles are similar.

Often the difficulty in a GMAT problem with similar triangles is simply recognizing that you are dealing with two similar triangles. Consider the following problem:

5.   In the following diagram DE is parallel to AC. If AC = 10 and DE = 5 and the area of triangle ABC is 40 then what is the area of triangle BDE?

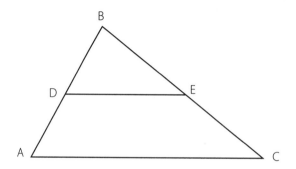

(A)   8

(B)   10

(C)   12

(D)   10√2

(E)   20

GMAT Insider: On harder triangle questions, be prepared to use your knowledge of similar triangles, triangles with supplementary angles, and the third side rule.

Geometry

Quadrilaterals

Quadrilaterals (four-sided figures) present some of the easier geometry material for the GMAT. Still, basic questions will seem very difficult if you do not memorize the necessary formulas. To show the importance of this memorization, consider the following questions:

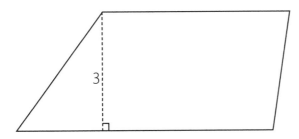

Note: Figure not drawn to scale.

6.   In the trapezoid above, the average length of the two parallel sides is 6. What is the area of the above trapezoid?

(A)   9

(B)   18

(C)   27

(D)   36

(E)   54

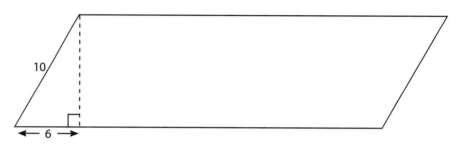

Note: Figure not drawn to scale.

7.   If the area of the parallelogram above is 360, what is its perimeter?

(A)   100

(B)   110

(C)   120

(D)   130

(E)   140

Facts & Formulas:
Area of a square: L^2
Perimeter of a square: $4L$
Area of a rectangle: $L \cdot W$
Perimeter of a rectangle: $2L + 2W$
Area of a parallelogram: $b \cdot h$
Perimeter of a parallelogram: $2a + 2b$
Area of a trapezoid: $\frac{1}{2}(b + c) \cdot h$
Perimeter of a trapezoid: $a + b + c + d$

The same question, but easier:

Note: Figure not drawn to scale.

If the area of the parallelogram above is 360, what is its perimeter ?

(A)   100

(B)   110

(C)   120

(D)   130

(E)   140

Think Like the Test Maker:
Geometry questions are often made more difficult by testing rules of multiple shapes. In particular, the GMAT loves right triangles.

GMAT Insider: Each of the major quadrilateral types is associated with right triangles. A square can be split into 2 isosceles right triangles. The diagonal of a rectangle likewise form right triangles. For trapezoids and parallelograms, a right triangle is often needed to find the height.

The Properties of Diagonals of Quadrilaterals

Some GMAT questions deal with the properties of the diagonals of common quadrilaterals. Let's examine those properties:

Diagonals of a square:
1. equal in length
2. intersect at 90º
3. bisect each other

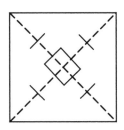

Diagonals of a rectangle:
1. equal in length
2. bisect each other

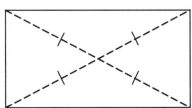

Diagonals of a rhombus:
1. intersect at 90º
2. bisect each other

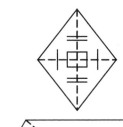

Diagonals of a parallelogram:
1. bisect each other

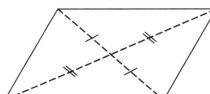

> **Facts & Formulas:**
> To bisect means to cut exactly in half.

8.   Is quadrilateral Q a square?

        (1)   The sides of Q have the same length.

        (2)   The diagonals of Q have the same length.

(A)   Statement (1) ALONE is sufficient, but statement (2) alone is not sufficient.

(B)   Statement (2) ALONE is sufficient, but statement (1) alone is not sufficient.

(C)   BOTH statements TOGETHER are sufficient, but NEITHER statement ALONE
         is sufficient.

(D)   EACH statement ALONE is sufficient.

(E)   Statements (1) and (2) TOGETHER are NOT sufficient

Other Polygons

All two-dimensional closed plane figures bounded by straight lines are called polygons. While the most common polygons on the GMAT are triangles and quadrilaterals, it is possible to see other multi-sided figures such as pentagons, hexagons, etc. To deal with these figures it is very important to know several important rules and definitions:

1.   The sum of the interior angles of any polygon is = (number of sides - 2)180.

> **Facts & Formula:** Sum of interior angles for any polygon = $(n-2)(180°)$ where n is the number of sides for that polygon.

Example: *What is the sum of the interior angles of a pentagon?*
(5-2)(180°) = 540°

Note
While it is useful to know this rule, you can also use your knowledge of triangles to determine the total of the interior angles of any polygon by dividing that polygon into triangles.

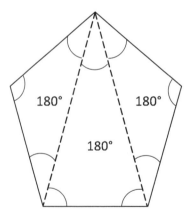

> **Facts & Formula:** In any regular polygon, you can find each angle by dividing the sum of the interior angles by the number of sides.

2.   A regular polygon is one where all sides and angles are exactly the same length and measure.

Example: *What is the measure of each angle in a regular pentagon?*
The sum of the angles is 540° and the number of sides is 5. Thus each angle in a regular pentagon has a measure of 108°.

Circles

On the GMAT, circle problems represent some of the harder geometry problems that students will face. In this section, we will review some of the definitions and formulas that students encountered in the Math Essentials. We will then look in more detail at some of the more challenging areas such as arcs, central angles, and inscribed angles.

Basics

As in arithmetic, it is essential that students are confident with their definitions in geometry. Do you remember what a sector is? How about a minor or major arc? Let's review these important circle definitions:

1. Radius

The **radius** of a circle describes the distance from the center of a circle to the circle itself.

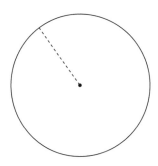

2. Diameter

The **diameter** of a circle describes the distance from one side of the circle to the other side, intersecting the center of the circle. **The diameter is twice the length of the radius.**

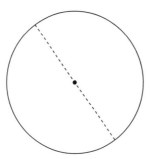

3. Chord

A line that connects any two points on a circle is known as a chord. The diameter of a circle is an example of a chord.

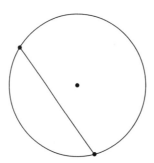

4. Circumference, Major Arcs, Minor Arcs

The circumference of a circle is defined as the boundary line that encloses that circle. An arc is defined as any portion of that circumference. When an arc is created by two variables as seen in the following diagram, the major arc is the larger arc and the minor arc is the smaller arc. In this example, major arc AB describes the longer dashed portion of the circumference and minor arc AB describes the shorter bold portion of the circumference:

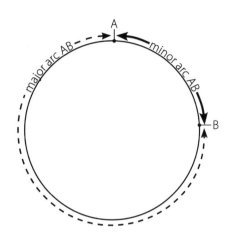

> **Facts & Formulas:** As you learned in Math Essentials, the circumference of a circle is given by the following formulas: $C = 2\pi r$ or πd. The area of a circle is given by: $A = \pi r^2$.

When three variables are used to describe an arc, it is not necessary to describe it as a major or minor arc. In this example, we can refer to the dashed portion of the circumference simply as arc ABC.

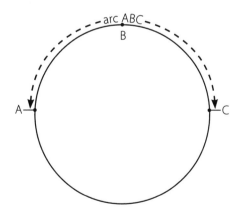

5. Central and Inscribed Angles

A **central angle** is any angle whose vertex (point of origin) is at the center of the circle. An **inscribed angle** is any angle whose vertex (point of origin) is on the circumference of a circle.

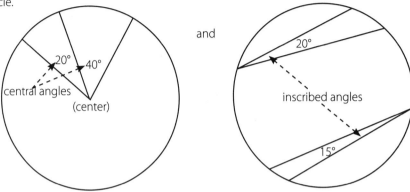

and

6. Sector

A **sector** is a portion of a circle defined by two radii and an arc carved by a central angle. In the following diagram, the bolded section would be described as sector ABCD.

How Your Mind Works: You can think of a sector as a slice of pizza.

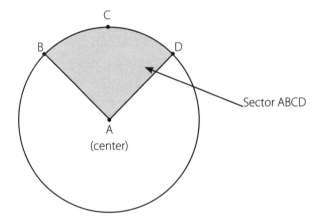

7. Tangent

A line that touches a circle at only one point on a circle is called a **tangent**. The tangent is perpendicular to the radius at the point of tangency.

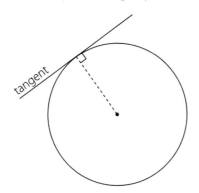

Additional Formulas and Properties of Circles

1. Arcs and Central Angles

Some of the more important properties of circles deal with the relationship between central angles and their corresponding arcs. Consider the following diagram:

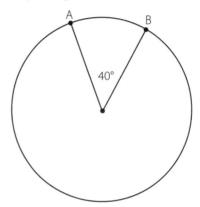

In this diagram we see that the central angle cutting out minor arc AB is equal to 40°. There is a direct relationship between that central angle and the arc that the angle subtends (cuts out). Because the central angles of a circle total 360° and the central angle in this example is 40°, we know that the minor arc AB must be $\frac{40}{360}$ or $\frac{1}{9}$th of the total circumference.

In any circle, the arc that is subtended (cut out) by a central angle relates to the circumference in the same proportion that the central angle relates to 360°.

> **Facts & Formula:**
>
> $$\frac{\text{Central Angle}}{360} = \frac{\text{Minor Arc}}{\text{Circumference}}$$

Consider the following GMAT question that tests arcs and central angles:

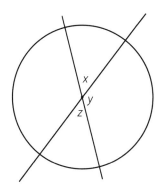

Note: Figure not drawn to scale.

9. x, y, and z are angles created by the two straight lines that intersect the center of the circle above. If $y - x = 100°$, what portion of the total circumference of the circle is made up by the arc of angle z?

(A) $\frac{1}{9}$

(B) $\frac{1}{6}$

(C) $\frac{5}{18}$

(D) $\frac{1}{3}$

(E) $\frac{7}{18}$

In addition to the unique relationship between arcs and their central angles there is also an important relationship between central angles, inscribed angles, and arcs.

2. Inscribed Angles

All inscribed angles that subtend (cut out) the same arc or arcs of equal length are equal in measure. In the following diagram, angles x, y, and z are all equal because they are inscribed angles that cut out minor arc AB: $x° = y° = z°$.

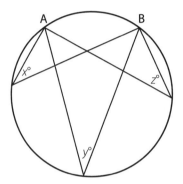

3. Inscribed Angles and Central Angles

Any inscribed angle that cuts out the same arc as a central angle is exactly one-half the measure of that central angle. In the following diagram, angles x, y, and z must all be 20° because they are cutting out the same minor arc AB as the 40° central angle.

$$x° = y° = z° = \frac{40°}{2} = 20°$$

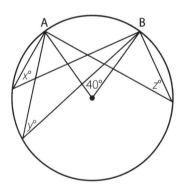

4. Inscribed Angles and Arcs

Because there is a distinct relationship between inscribed angles and central angles, we can use our previous knowledge to determine any arc that is cut out by an inscribed angle.

To determine an arc from an inscribed angle, simply draw in the central angle (which will always be twice the measure of the inscribed angle) and use the arc/central angle proportion to determine the length of the arc.

In the following figure what is the length of minor arc AB?

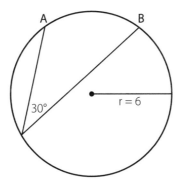

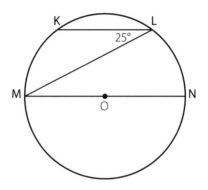

10.   In the circle above, MN has a length of 12 and KL is parallel to MN. What is the length of the minor arc KL?

(A)   2π

(B) $\frac{8\pi}{3}$

(C)   8π

(D)   32π

(E)   36π

5. Triangles Inscribed in a Circle

If A and B are two endpoints on a circle's diameter and C is a point anywhere on the circumference of the circle, then the triangle ABC is a right triangle with C as the right angle.

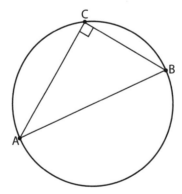

Example: *What is the area of the circle above if BC has length 3 and the angle CAB is 30°?*

The first thing to look for when dealing with triangle problems is whether the triangle matches one of the common triangles we reviewed earlier. We see that this is a triangle with angles of 30°, 60°, 90°, which means that its sides have proportions $1 : \sqrt{3} : 2$. Hence, AB is $3 \cdot 2 = 6$ and the radius of the circle is therefore 3. The area of the circle is $\pi 3^2 = 9\pi$.

In addition to this important property, there are many other problems where other figures are inscribed within circles or circles are inscribed within other figures. In the homework, you will do several circle problems that combine your knowledge of equilateral triangles, 30-60-90 triangles, and circles.

Try the following difficult geometry problem that incorporates several concepts previously discussed:

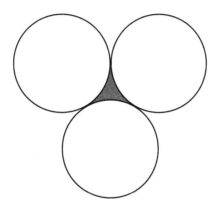

11.   Three identical circles of circumference 12π are each tangent to one another at exactly one point. What is the area of the shaded region ?

(A) $9\sqrt{3} - 18\,\pi$

(B) $18\sqrt{3} - 12\,\pi$

(C) $36\sqrt{3} - 36\,\pi$

(D) $36\sqrt{3} - 18\,\pi$

(E) $36\sqrt{3} - 6\,\pi$

GMAT Insider: When encountering a difficult Geometry question, look exclusively for the shapes that you are responsible for. Difficult Geometry questions will often require test takers to find a common shape where it is not explicitly drawn or referenced, such as the diagonal of a rectangle forming a right triangle.

The same question, slightly easier:

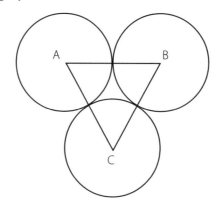

Think Like the Test Maker: The GMAT derives all of its questions from the core concepts you will learn in this course, and has a few standard methods for making them more difficult. One is to add multiple steps in the process. Another is to obscure the concept being tested – here there was no mention of a triangle, but the triangle was a crucial component. When faced with a difficult question, be prepared to efficiently handle multiple intermediate steps, and remember that the concepts to be tested are those that you have already studied; you may, however, need to apply concepts that may not seem to be relevant at first.

A triangle is formed by connecting the centers of three identical, tangent circles as shown above. Each circle has a radius of 6. What is the area of triangle ABC ?

(A) 18

(B) $18\sqrt{3}$

(C) 36

(D) $36\sqrt{3}$

(E) $72\sqrt{3}$

Lazy Genius: On Geometry questions, when it appears that a concept may be hidden, try to find an opportunity to use your knowledge of right triangles.

Volumes and 3D Figures

On the GMAT, most three dimensional figure questions involve the following common 3D figures: cubes, rectangular solids, and cylinders. Occasionally, the GMAT will ask questions on cones, spheres, and other less common figures. Whenever the question involves a figure where the volume cannot be calculated with the information you have learned so far, you will be provided with volume equations for those figures. Let's look first at the common 3D Figures:

Volume for Common 3D Figures

For any three dimensional figure that has a known base (a rectangle, circle, triangle, etc.) and a height that is perpendicular to that base, the volume is found by multiplying the area of the base by the height. In a rectangular solid the base is arbitrary (in other words, pick a base and make the remaining dimension the height). Consider the following diagrams:

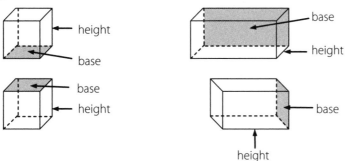

For any other solid, put the common figure as the base and the height will be the straight line dimension that is perpendicular to that base. Consider the following diagrams:

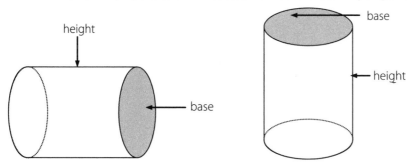

Find the volumes for the following three figures:

1. Rectangular Solid

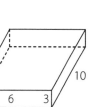

2. Right Cylinder

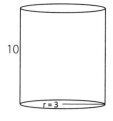

3. Triangular Solid

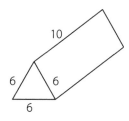

Facts & Formula:
Volume = (Area of the base) x (Height)

1. For the rectangular solid, simply multiply the length times the width to get the area of the base (60) and multiply that times the height (3) to get the volume of 180.

2. For the cylinder, find the area of the circle that forms the base: $3^2\pi = 9\pi$ and multiply that times the height (10) to get the volume of 90π.

3. For the triangular solid, make the triangle the base and find its area. Since the triangle is equilateral, you can use the formula for the area of an equilateral triangle $\frac{s^2\sqrt{3}}{4}$ to quickly determine the area of the base = $9\sqrt{3}$. Multiply that times the height of 10 to get the volume of $90\sqrt{3}$.

Definitions for Common 3D Figures

Before examining surface area, it is important that students are comfortable with several other definitions relating to 3D figures. The most important definitions relate to rectangular solids and are indicated in the following diagram:

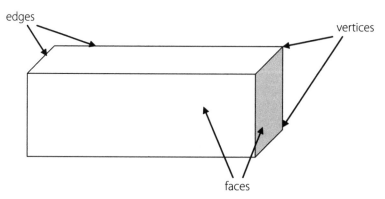

Students should also remember the units of measurements for area vs. volume:

Surface Area for Common 3D Figures

Surface area is a measure of the total area of all faces of a three dimensional figure. Almost all surface area questions on the GMAT involve rectangular solids. For any rectangular solid there are 6 faces. When the dimensions (length, width, and height) are all different then there are 3 unique surfaces – the front and the back are the same, the top and the bottom are the same, and the two sides are the same. Therefore the surface area for any rectangular solid can be written as $2lw + 2lh + 2wh$ where $2lw$ represents the top and bottom, $2lh$ represents the two sides, and $2wh$ represents the front and back. In more specialized rectangular solids such as a cube, you can simplify this formula because all the dimensions are the same.

For figures other than rectangular solids, it is not necessary to memorize specific formulas. Rather, you should use your knowledge of basic geometry and the definition of surface area to reason out the answer. To practice this, calculate the surface area for the same three figures that we used for volume:

> **Facts & Formulas:**
> Distance is measured in inches, feet, yards, miles, etc.
> Area is measured in inches^2, feet^2, yards^2, miles^2, etc.
> Volume is measured in inches^3, feet^3, yards^3, miles^3, etc.

> **Facts & Formulas:**
> Surface area for rectangular solid = $2lw + 2lh + 2wh$
> Surface area for a cube = $6s^2$ where s is the single dimension and volume for a cube = s^3.

> *How Your Mind Works:* When finding the surface area of the side of a cylinder, think of it as taking the label off a tin can.

1. Rectangular Solid

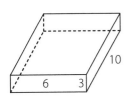

2. Right Cylinder

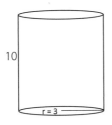

3. Triangular Solid

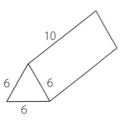

1. For the rectangular box, simply plug in the dimensions to the formula that we have learned.
$SA = 2(6)(10) + 2(3)(10) + 2(6)(3) = 216$

2. For the cylinder, the exercise is a bit more difficult. First find the area of the top and the bottom of the cylinder. Each circle has an area of $3^2\pi = 9\pi$ so the top and the bottom together have a surface area of 18π. Next you must calculate the surface area of the cylindrical portion of the cylinder. If you simply unravel that portion, it is actually a rectangle with a width of 10 (the height of the cylinder) and a length that is equal to the circumference of the circle

> *GMAT Insider:* There is no direct relationship between volume and surface area for rectangular solids unless it is a cube. In other words, if you are told that the volume of a rectangular solid has doubled, it is not possible to calculate the change in surface area unless the change to each of the dimensions is given.

that forms the base. The circumference is equal to $2\pi(3) = 6\pi$ so the area of the rectangle is $6\pi(10)$ or 60π. The total surface area of the cylinder is then $60\pi + 18\pi = 78\pi$.

3. For the triangular solid, take the area of the equilateral triangles on the top and the bottom. That area is $9\sqrt{3}$ so together the area of the top and bottom is $18\sqrt{3}$. The rest of the figure can be divided into three rectangles with width 6 and length of 10 and each having an area of 60. Therefore the total surface area of the figure is $180 + 18\sqrt{3}$.

Let's look at a full GMAT question testing surface area and volume:

12.   Employees at a steel plant want to determine how much water will fill a large steel tank in the shape of a rectangular box. What is the volume of this tank in cubic feet?

(1)   The height of the tank is 25 feet.

(2)   The total surface area of the tank is 3,300 square feet.

(A)   Statement (1) ALONE is sufficient, but statement (2) alone is not sufficient.

(B)   Statement (2) ALONE is sufficient, but statement (1) alone is not sufficient.

(C)   BOTH statements TOGETHER are sufficient, but NEITHER statement ALONE is sufficient.

(D)   EACH statement ALONE is sufficient.

(E)   Statements (1) and (2) TOGETHER are NOT sufficient.

Greatest Possible Distance in a Rectangular Box

One very common question type is finding the greatest possible distance within a rectangular box. Try the following problem:

> **Facts & Formula:** The greatest possible distance within any rectangular box $= \sqrt{l^2 + w^2 + h^2}$. If the figure is a cube, then all the dimensions are the same and the formula can be simplified to $\sqrt{3l^2}$. It is not required to memorize this formula – you can always derive the answer using Pythagorean theorem – but some students have found that memorization saves precious time on the test.

13.   A cube has a volume of 125 cm³. What is the longest possible straight line distance between two corners of the cube?

(A) $5\sqrt{2}$

(B) $5\sqrt{3}$

(C)   10

(D) $10\sqrt{2}$

(E)   20

Unusual 3D Figures

There is no limit to the type of figure that you might find in a three-dimensional GMAT problem. Just be assured that if the figure requires knowledge outside of the common 3D figures, you will be given the formula. The most common unusual figures used on the GMAT are cones and spheres. In the homework, you will encounter several difficult problems testing unusual 3D figures.

> *Habits of Great Test Takers:* As a former athlete, I try to approach the test like I would a big game – each question is a fresh play, and I need to be ready for 40+ questions in a 75-minute competition. That mentality allows me to realize that, each time I conquer one battle, I'm looking forward to the next, and I'm one step closer to enjoying the spoils of victory. I may not win every single play, but as long as I attack each to the best of my ability and move on to the next with a fresh mind and proactive approach, I know I can win the game.
>
> – Jeff Robinson, Moscow

Coordinate Geometry

Coordinate geometry is an area of increasing importance on the GMAT. Students are reporting that they have faced multiple questions on coordinate geometry on their tests. To be prepared for these questions, students must relearn the basic concepts associated with coordinate geometry and then be able to quickly apply some of the formulas and properties that are addressed at the end of this chapter. To start, let's review the definitions and properties of lines in the coordinate geometry plane:

Lines in the Coordinate Geometry Plane:

All algebraic equations that are linear (have no exponents greater than 1) can be mapped on the coordinate geometry plane as a straight line. It is easiest to map that line on the coordinate geometry plane when the equation is in the following form:

$$y = mx + b$$

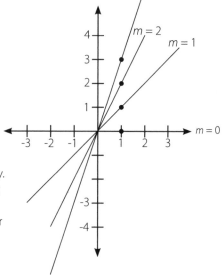

1. Slope

In the equation $y = mx + b$, m describes the slope of the line.

The higher m is, the steeper the line. This can be seen by setting $b = 0$ and trying different values for m. If $m = 1, 2$, or 3, then we have equations $y = x$, $y = 2x$, and $y = 3x$, respectively. When $x = 0$, $y = 0$ in all of these equations. But when $x = 1$, the equations with the bigger slope (the higher values of m) will have higher values for y, as seen in the diagram at right. The slope of a line can be found by:

$$\frac{\text{change in } y \text{ coordinate}}{\text{change in } x \text{ coordinate}} = \frac{y_2 - y_1}{x_2 - x_1} = \text{slope}$$

If the slope has a positive value, the line will be pointing up to the right.
If the slope has a negative value, the line will be pointing down to the right.

What is the slope of the line in this diagram?

$$\frac{\text{change in } y \text{ coordinate}}{\text{change in } x \text{ coordinate}} = \text{slope}$$

$$\frac{10 - (-20)}{20 - (-40)} = \frac{30}{60} = \frac{1}{2} = 0.5$$

2. *x* and *y* intercepts

In the equation $y = mx + b$, b describes the intersection with the *y*-axis, known as the **y-intercept**.

The higher b is, the higher up the line intersects the *y*-axis. Again, this can be seen by setting $m = 1$ and $x = 0$, and trying different values for b.

The point where the line intersects the *x*-axis is called the **x-intercept**. The *x*-intercept can be found by setting $y = 0$.

The equation $y = mx + b$ descibes a straight line with the following properties:

y-intercept $= b$ x-intercept $= -\frac{b}{m}$ slope $= m$

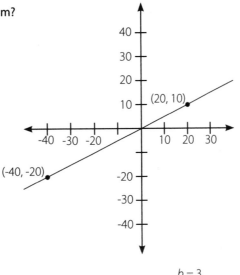

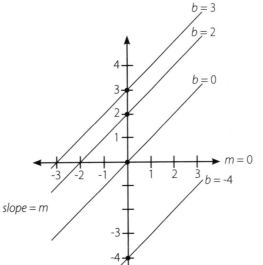

GMAT Insider: The ability to quickly find *x* and *y* intercepts is one of the most important skills for coordinate geometry.

Coordinate Geometry Drill

To better understand these basic coordinate geometry concepts, let's look at some quick questions drilling this knowledge.

1. If a line has a positive slope, which two quadrants must the line pass through? What if it has a negative slope? Give the equation for a line that passes through only quadrants I and II.

2. Find the point where $y = 3x + 5$ and $y = -2x - 10$ intersect.

3. What are the equations for the y-axis and the x-axis?

4. Arrange the following equations in ascending order based on the value of their x- intercepts. Do the same for their y-intercepts.

A. $6 + 12x = 3y$
B. $x + 2y = 8$
C. $15x + 5y + 10 = 0$

5. What is the area of the triangle formed by the intersection of $y = 2x - 2$, $y = -\frac{1}{2}x + 8$, and $y = 0$?

Important Properties and Formulas for Difficult Coordinate Geometry Problems (Self Study)

Now that we have reviewed the basic definitions and equations for use on the coordinate geometry plane, let's look at some important properties and formulas that allow you to solve even the hardest coordinate geometry questions quickly.

1. Distance Formula

To find the distance between two points on the coordinate plane, you will need to use the Pythagorean theorem you learned in the Triangles section.

To find the distance from the origin (which is point 0,0) to A, we take advantage of the fact that the line between the two points forms the hypotenuse in a right angled triangle.

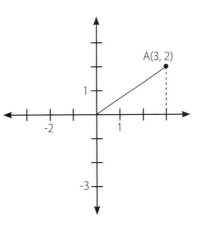

We see that one side has a length of 3 and the other has a length of 2, and we know that $2^2 + 3^2 = c^2$. Therefore $c = \sqrt{2^2 + 3^2} = \sqrt{13}$ and the distance between the two points is determined.

The work done above can be simplified with a general formula for finding the distance between any two points:
$\sqrt{(x_1 - x_2)^2 + (y_1 - y_2)^2}$

Example: *What is the distance between points (3,8) and (9,16) on the coordinate geometry plane?*

By using Pythagorean theory, you can see that the triangle formed with these points is a 6, 8,10 right triangle so the missing piece – the hypotenuse – is 10. Or you can plug into the formula above to get the same result.

> **Facts & Formula:** The distance between any two points (x_1, y_1) and $(x_2, y_2) = \sqrt{(x_1 - x_2)^2 + (y_1 - y_2)^2}$

> ***GMAT Insider:*** Knowing how to calculate the distance between two points on the coordinate geometry plane is an essential skill for the GMAT. Students should either memorize this formula or simply use Pythagorean thereom to determine the distance. However, memorizing the formula is strictly optional. If you understand how to use the Pythagorean theorem, the formula is unnecessary, though it may save you a few seconds on the test.

2. Midpoint Formula

On some GMAT problems it is essential to find the midpoint between any two points. While not nearly as important as the distance formula, the midpoint formula could be an important part of a difficult GMAT coordinate geometry question.

Consider the following GMAT question:

14. Which of the following points is exactly halfway between (3,9) and (5,-3)?

(A)   (4,6)

(B)   (4,3)

(C)   (6,4)

(D)   (2,12)

(E)   (2,6)

Facts & Formula: The midpoint between any two points (x_1, y_1) and (x_2, y_2) in the coordinate plane is found by taking the average of the x and y coordinates.

Thus the midpoint $= \left(\dfrac{x_1 + x_2}{2}, \dfrac{y_1 + y_2}{2} \right)$

GMAT Insider: Without knowing the midpoint formula, problems such as this are timeconsuming and tedious. Students who know the formula can apply it and quickly answer this type of difficult question.

3. Slopes of Parallel Lines

In the coordinate geometry plane, lines that are parallel will always have the same slope. In the following diagram consider these 3 lines that all have the same slope of 1.

$y = x + 2$
$y = x - 2$
$y = x$

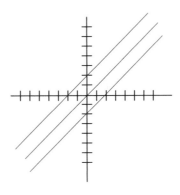

4. Slopes of Perpendicular Lines

In the coordinate geometry plane, lines that are perpendicular will have slopes that are the negative reciprocals of each other. In other words, if the product of the slopes of two lines is -1, then they are perpendicular to each other. Consider the following diagram that shows the following two lines:

$y = -\frac{1}{2}x + 2$ and $y = 2x + 4$

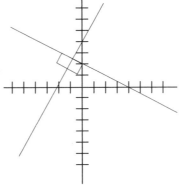

Because the slopes of these two lines are negative reciprocals of each other, we know that the intersection is at ninety degrees.

5. Determing the Equation of a Line
   ## on the Coordinate Geometry Plane

For many GMAT questions, it is useful to know the minimum information required to determine the equation of a line in the coordinate geometry plane. If you are given any of the following it is possible to determine the equation of the line:

A. Any two points on the line.
B. One point on the line and the slope.
C. One point on the line and the slope or equation of a line perpendicular to that line.
D. One point on the line and the slope or equation of a line parallel to that line.

Example:
Provide the equation of a line that passes through points (2, 4) and (-4, -8).

The first step in this problem is to determine the slope which is the $\frac{\text{change in } y}{\text{change in } x}$ and in this example $\frac{12}{6} = 2$. Once you have the slope, you can simply use the slope equation again to get the equation of the line. This time use one of the given points, say (2, 4), as your first point, and use (x, y) as your other point. Then the slope equation will be $2 = \frac{(4 - y)}{(2 - x)}$. Solving for y we find that the equation of the line is simply $y=2x$.

5. Circles and Curved Lines in the Coordinate Geometry Plane

While not common, circles and curved lines are sometimes used on GMAT coordinate geometry problems. If you are ever faced with an equation that is not linear (in other words contains squared variables), simply use an input/output method to determine what the figure will look like on the coordinate geometry plane.

Try plugging in the following values for x in the equation and drawing the curved line on the coordinate plane.

$y = x^2 - x - 2$

x	-2	-1	-0.5	0	0.5	1	1.5	2	3
y									

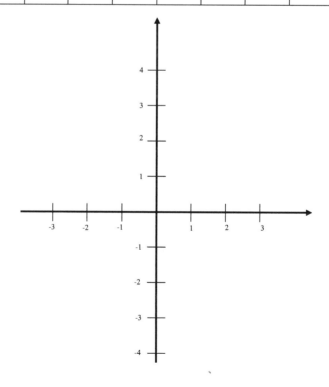

As you can see in that diagram, quadratics will produce curved lines and the graphical representation explains why there are can be two solutions in a quadratic equation. In addition to quadratics, you may see the equations for circles used on the GMAT. Any circle will be of the form $x^2 + y^2 =$ constant, $x^4 + y^4 =$ constant, etc. Consider the equation $x^2 + y^2 = 4$. The maximum value for either x or y is 2 and the graph of this equation looks like the following:

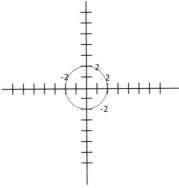

When you are dealing with circles or curved lines in the coordinate geometry plane, use your conceptual understanding of coordinate geometry to solve the problem (in other words, in a circle, the x-intercept is still on the line $y = 0$, – but there may be two x-intercepts). In the challenge problems, you will see several problems that deal with unusual figures in the coordinate geometry plane.

Assorted Problems

In the previous two books, problems were organized by question type so that students could become more proficient at each type. However, in geometry the most important skill is figuring out which rules to apply to a particular problem. In the lesson section, each set of rules was accompanied by an example problem to show how the information is tested on the GMAT. In the following problems, students must decide which geometry rules to apply and then use them properly to find a solution. Remember that many hard geometry problems start with geometry rules and then turn into difficult algebra problems. The first section is a collection of easy to moderate questions and the final section is a collection of difficult challenge problems.

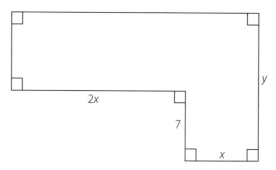

15.   The figure above has a perimeter of 50.
        Which of the following expresses y correctly in terms of x?

(A) $\frac{14}{3} + \frac{50}{3x}$

(B) $2 + \frac{25}{x}$

(C) $43 - 7x$

(D) $25 - 3x$

(E)   None of the above.

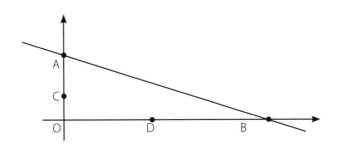

<u>Note</u>: Figure not drawn to scale.

16.   A line in a coordinate system is graphed by $y = -0.5x + 2$. Which of the following equations will yield a graph such that the area of triangle COD will be half the size of triangle AOB?

        I. $y = -0.25x + 1$
        II. $y = -0.25x + 2$
        III. $y = -x + 2$

(A)   I only

(B)   II only

(C)   III only

(D)   I and II only

(E)   I and III only

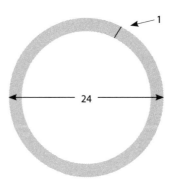

Note: Figure not drawn to scale.

17.   A gas-pipe has an outside diameter of 24 inches. The steel wall of the pipe is 1 inch thick. What is the area of the cross-section of the steel wall of the pipe?

(A)   23π

(B)   47π

(C)   143π

(D)   529π

(E)   575π

18.   If the width, depth, and length of a rectangular box were each decreased by 50%, by how many percent would the volume of the box decrease?

(A)   12.5%

(B)   25%

(C)   50%

(D)   75%

(E)   87.5%

19.   A pyramid with four equal-sized flat surfaces and a base of 36 feet² has a height of 10 feet. What is the total surface area of the pyramid, excluding the base?

(A) $12\sqrt{31}$

(B) $12\sqrt{109}$

(C) $24\sqrt{31}$

(D) $24\sqrt{109}$

(E) $48\sqrt{31}$

20. A rectangle is defined to be "silver" if and only if the ratio of its length to its width is 2 to 1. If rectangle S is silver, is rectangle R silver?

   (1)   R has the same area as S.

   (2)   The ratio of one side of R to one side of S is 2 to 1.

(A)   Statement (1) ALONE is sufficient, but statement (2) alone is not sufficient.

(B)   Statement (2) ALONE is sufficient, but statement (1) alone is not sufficient.

(C)   BOTH statements TOGETHER are sufficient, but NEITHER statement ALONE is sufficient.

(D)   EACH statement ALONE is sufficient.

(E)   Statements (1) and (2) TOGETHER are NOT sufficient.

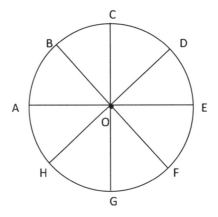

21.   A pizza with diameter of 12 inches is split into eight equally sized pieces. Four non-adjacent pieces are removed. What is the perimeter AOBCODEOFGOHA of the pizza now, including the inside edges of the slices?

(A)   48π + 48

(B)   24π + 48

(C)   24π + 24

(D)   6π + 48

(E)   6π + 24

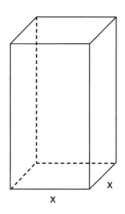

22.   A three dimensional "skeleton" rectangular shape is made up of metal rods. The rods' total length is 480. The base is a square with sides of length x. Which of the following expresses the height?

(A)   960 – 16x

(B)   480 – 8x

(C)   240 – 4x

(D)   120 – 2x

(E)   60 – x

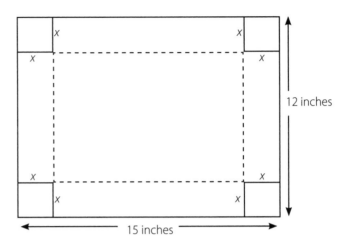

12 inches

15 inches

23. A rectangular flat sheet of metal is to be converted into an open box. To do this, four squares with sides *x* must be cut off. What value of *x* would yield a box with the greatest volume?

(A) 5

(B) 4

(C) 3

(D) 2

(E) 1

24. A cylinder with a volume of 54π has the same height and diameter. What is its diameter?

(A)   6

(B)   9

(C)   12

(D)   18

(E)   24

25.   A circle has an area of *y*. What is the length of its diameter in terms of *y*?

(A) $\sqrt{\dfrac{y}{\pi}}$

(B) $\sqrt{\dfrac{\pi}{y}}$

(C) $\sqrt{\dfrac{2y}{\pi}}$

(D) $2\sqrt{\dfrac{y}{\pi}}$

(E) $2\sqrt{\dfrac{\pi}{y}}$

26.   A circle is considered large if it has an area greater than 25.
       Is circle C with center on the origin considered large?

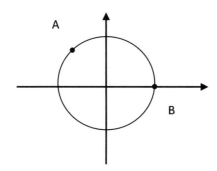

       (1)   The coordinates of point A are (-3, 4)

       (2)   The coordinates of point B are (5, 0)

(A)   Statement (1) ALONE is sufficient, but statement (2) alone is not sufficient.

(B)   Statement (2) ALONE is sufficient, but statement (1) alone is not sufficient.

(C)   BOTH statements TOGETHER are sufficient, but NEITHER statement ALONE
       is sufficient.

(D)   EACH statement ALONE is sufficient.

(E)   Statements (1) and (2) TOGETHER are NOT sufficient.

27.   If the *x*-coordinate of point E is 4, what is its *y*-coordinate?

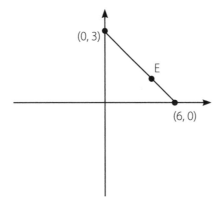

(A) $-\frac{1}{2}$

(B)   1

(C) $\frac{3}{2}$

(D)   2

(E) $\frac{7}{2}$

28. Starting from Town S, Fred rode his bicycle 8 miles due east, 3 miles due south, 2 miles due west, and 11 miles due north, finally stopping at Town T. If the entire region is flat, what is the straight-line distance, in miles, between Towns S and T ?

(A) 10

(B) $8\sqrt{2}$

(C) $\sqrt{157}$

(D) 14

(E) 24

29. Rex has a 24 ft² sheet of wood and cuts it into 6 identical square pieces (with no pieces of wood left over). He uses these pieces to make a box. How much dirt can this wood box hold (in ft³)?

(A)   1

(B)   4

(C)   8

(D)   16

(E)   24

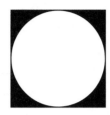

30.   The figure above represents the floor of a square foyer with a circular rug partially covering the floor and extending to the outer edges of the floor as shown. What is the area of the foyer floor that is not covered by the rug?

     (1)   The area of the foyer is 9 square meters.

     (2)   The area of the rug is 2.25π square meters.

(A)   Statement (1) ALONE is sufficient, but statement (2) alone is not sufficient.

(B)   Statement (2) ALONE is sufficient, but statement (1) alone is not sufficient.

(C)   BOTH statements TOGETHER are sufficient, but NEITHER statement ALONE is sufficient.

(D)   EACH statement ALONE is sufficient.

(E)   Statements (1) and (2) TOGETHER are NOT sufficient.

31. Which of the following points falls outside of the region defined by $2y \leq 6x - 12$?

(A)   (5, 1)

(B)   (3, -8)

(C)   (2, 0)

(D)   (1, -2)

(E)   (0, -14)

32. The size of a television screen is given as the length of the screen's diagonal. If the screens were flat, then the area of a square 21-inch screen would be how many square inches greater than the area of a square 19-inch screen?

(A)   2

(B)   4

(C)   16

(D)   38

(E)   40

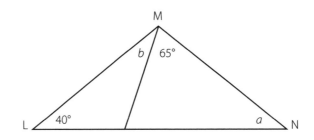

33.   In triangle LMN above, what is *b* in terms of *a*?

(A) $a - 105$

(B) $75 - a$

(C) $a - 75$

(D) $105 + a$

(E) $105 - a$

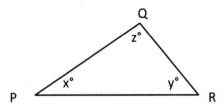

34.   In ΔPQR above is PQ > RP?

    (1) $x = y$

    (2) $y = z$

(A)   Statement (1) ALONE is sufficient, but statement (2) alone is not sufficient.

(B)   Statement (2) ALONE is sufficient, but statement (1) alone is not sufficient.

(C)   BOTH statements TOGETHER are sufficient, but NEITHER statement ALONE is sufficient.

(D)   EACH statement ALONE is sufficient.

(E)   Statements (1) and (2) TOGETHER are NOT sufficient.

35. In three-dimensional space, if each of the two lines L1 and L2 is perpendicular to line L3, which of the following must be true?

(I.)   L1 is parallel to L2
(II.)   L1 is perpendicular to L2
(III.) L1 and L2 lie on the same plane

(A)   I only

(B)   I and II

(C)   II and III

(D)   III only

(E)   none of the above

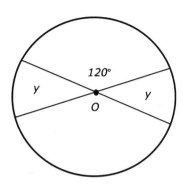

36.   The two regions marked with the letter y comprise what fraction of the circle
        above with center O?

(A)   1

(B) $\frac{1}{2}$

(C) $\frac{1}{3}$

(D) $\frac{1}{6}$

(E) $\frac{1}{12}$

37. A soft-drink producer has done marketing research and found that if it decreases the width of its soda cans (right circular cylinders) by 50%, but keep the height the same, they can still sell the cans for 75% of the original price. By what percent does the price per volume of soda increase to the consumer?

(A)   25%

(B)   50%

(C)   100%

(D)   200%

(E)   300%

38.   What is the perimeter of triangle PQR?

    (1)   The measures of angles PQR, QRP, and RPQ are $x°$, $2x°$, and $3x°$, respectively.

    (2)   The altitude of triangle PQR from Q to PR is 4.

(A)   Statement (1) ALONE is sufficient, but statement (2) alone is not sufficient.

(B)   Statement (2) ALONE is sufficient, but statement (1) alone is not sufficient.

(C)   BOTH statements TOGETHER are sufficient, but NEITHER statement ALONE is sufficient.

(D)   EACH statement ALONE is sufficient.

(E)   Statements (1) and (2) TOGETHER are NOT sufficient.

39.   A cylinder is being filled with sand weighing 200 kg. per cubic foot. The cylinder
       has a diameter of 1 foot and is 5 feet tall. How much sand is being used?

(A)   250π kg.

(B)   500π kg.

(C)   500π² kg.

(D)   1000π kg.

(E)   1000π² kg.

40.   Is the figure shown above a rectangle?

(1) $c = d$

(2) $c + d = 180$

(A)   Statement (1) ALONE is sufficient, but statement (2) alone is not sufficient.

(B)   Statement (2) ALONE is sufficient, but statement (1) alone is not sufficient.

(C)   BOTH statements TOGETHER are sufficient, but NEITHER statement ALONE is sufficient.

(D)   EACH statement ALONE is sufficient.

(E)   Statements (1) and (2) TOGETHER are NOT sufficient.

41.   A circle and a square have the same area. The square's sides are 4 feet long. What is the radius of the circle?

(A) $\dfrac{\sqrt{2}}{\sqrt{\pi}}$

(B) $\dfrac{2}{\sqrt{\pi}}$

(C) $\dfrac{2}{\pi}$

(D) $\dfrac{4}{\sqrt{\pi}}$

(E) $\dfrac{4}{\pi}$

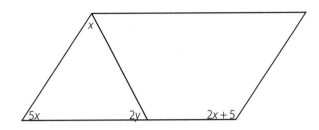

Note: Figure not drawn to scale.

42.   In the parallelogram above, what is the value of y?

(A)   10

(B)   15

(C)   20

(D)   35

(E)   45

43. A product designer is trying to design the largest container possible that will fit in a 6 x 12 x 14 box. Because of constraints in the manufacturing process, he must make the container in the shape of a cylinder, which will then be placed base down inside the box. What is the volume of the largest cylinder that can fit in the box?

(A) 108π

(B) 126π

(C) 216π

(D) 504π

(E) 864π

44.   What fractional part of the total surface area of cube C is red?

(1)   Each of 3 faces of C is exactly $\frac{1}{2}$ red.

(2)   Each of 3 faces of C is entirely white.

(A)   Statement (1) ALONE is sufficient, but statement (2) alone is not sufficient.

(B)   Statement (2) ALONE is sufficient, but statement (1) alone is not sufficient.

(C)   BOTH statements TOGETHER are sufficient, but NEITHER statement ALONE is sufficient.

(D)   EACH statement ALONE is sufficient.

(E)   Statements (1) and (2) TOGETHER are NOT sufficient.

45. What is the greatest distance between two points in a cylinder where the area of the base is 9π and the height is 5?

(A) $\sqrt{34}$

(B) $\sqrt{48}$

(C) $\sqrt{61}$

(D) $\sqrt{76}$

(E) $\sqrt{106}$

46.   If the radius of a circle doubles, by what factor does the area increase?

(A)   2

(B)   4

(C)   2π

(D)   4π

(E)   4π²

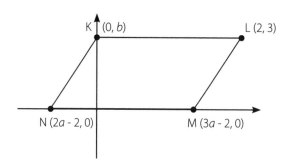

47.   In the rectangular coordinate system above, the area of parallelogram KLMN is

(A) $\dfrac{6}{\sqrt{3}}$

(B)   6

(C) $6\sqrt{3}$

(D)   12

(E)   Cannot be determined

48.   If a large pizza has a radius that is 30 percent larger than that of a medium pizza, what is the percent increase in area between a medium and a large pizza?

(A)   30 %

(B)   36 %

(C)   60 %

(D)   69 %

(E)   90 %

49.   If the area of triangular region RST is 25, what is the perimeter of RST?

    (1)   The length of one side of RST is $5\sqrt{2}$.

    (2)   RST is a right isosceles triangle.

    (A)   Statement (1) ALONE is sufficient, but statement (2) alone is not sufficient.

    (B)   Statement (2) ALONE is sufficient, but statement (1) alone is not sufficient.

    (C)   BOTH statements TOGETHER are sufficient, but NEITHER statement ALONE is sufficient.

    (D)   EACH statement ALONE is sufficient.

    (E)   Statements (1) and (2) TOGETHER are NOT sufficient.

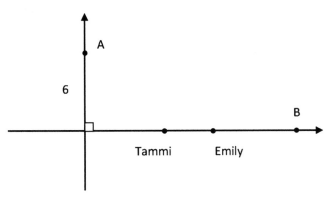

50.   Emily and Tammi must both run from point A to reach the finish line, which
       stretches from the origin to point B, but they have to run on two different paths,
       where Emily will end up 4 yards away from Tammi on the finish line. If Tammi ran
       a total of 10 yards, how many yards more did Emily run than Tammi?

(A)   2

(B) $4\sqrt{2}-10$

(C) $6\sqrt{5}-10$

(D) $4\sqrt{2}-8$

(E) $6\sqrt{5}$

51. A dog is tied to the corner of a fence with an 9 foot chain. If the angle of that corner of the fence is 120 degrees, how many square feet does the dog have to walk around (The dog is tied inside, not outside, the fence)?

(A) 19π

(B) 27

(C) 27π

(D) 81

(E) 81π

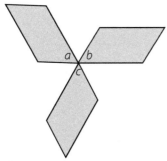

Note: Figure not drawn to scale

52.   If each of the line segments in the figure above has a length equal to 4, and the angles *a*, *b*, and *c* are each 60 degrees, what is the total area of the shaded figures?

(A)   16

(B) $8\sqrt{3}$

(C) $24\sqrt{2}$

(D)   36

(E) $24\sqrt{3}$

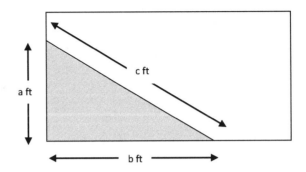

53.   The shaded portion of the rectangular yard shown above represents a wooden patio. If the area of the patio is 30 square feet and $b = a + 7$, then c equals

(A) $\sqrt{2}$

(B) $2\sqrt{2}$

(C)   5

(D)   12

(E)   13

54. A deli sells soup, priced by weight, in two sizes of right circular cylindrical plastic containers. The height and the radius of size A are each three times that of size B. If a customer fills a size B container of soup to capacity, and pays $2, how much would a size A container filled to half of its capacity cost?

(A) $9

(B) $12

(C) $18

(D) $21

(E) $27

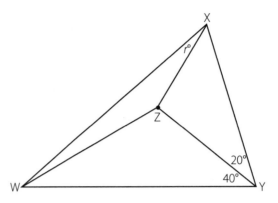

Note: Figure not drawn to scale.

55.   In the figure above, ZW = ZX = ZY. What is the value of *r*?

(A)   30

(B)   50

(C)   70

(D)   90

(E)   120

56.   In a rectangle the shortest side is 4 inches shorter than the longest. The area of
       the rectangle is 252 square inches. How long is the longest side of the rectangle?

(A)   12

(B)   14

(C)   16

(D)   18

(E)   20

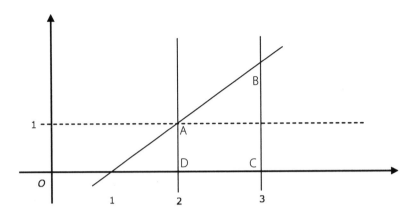

57.   In the rectangular coordinate system above, the quadrilateral ABCD is bounded by straight lines. Which of the following is NOT an equation of one of the boundary lines?

(A) $y = 0$

(B) $x = 2$

(C) $x = 3$

(D) $y - x = -1$

(E) $y + 2x = -\dfrac{1}{2}$

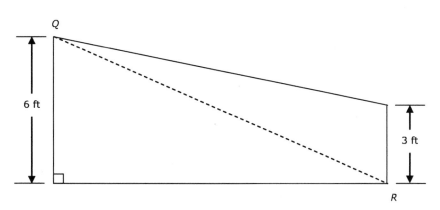

58.   The trapezoid shown in the figure above represents a cross section of a large piece of wood that will be used in the construction of a house. If the distance from Q to R is 10 feet, what is the area of the cross section of the piece of wood in square feet?

(A)   30

(B)   33

(C)   36

(D)   40

(E)   45.5

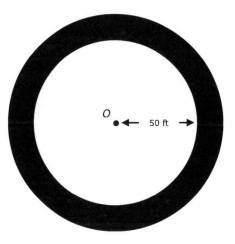

59.   The figure above shows a circular auditorium, with its center at O, surrounded by a small ring-shaped seating section that is 10 feet wide. What is the area of the seating section, in square feet?

(A)   100π

(B)   730π

(C)   1,000π

(D)   1,100π

(E)   1,500π

Challenge Problems

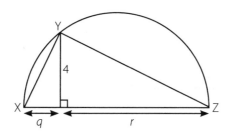

60.   If arc XYZ above is a semicircle, what is its length?

(1) $q = 2$

(2) $r = 8$

(A)   Statement (1) ALONE is sufficient, but statement (2) alone is not sufficient.

(B)   Statement (2) ALONE is sufficient, but statement (1) alone is not sufficient.

(C)   BOTH statements TOGETHER are sufficient, but NEITHER statement ALONE is sufficient.

(D)   EACH statement ALONE is sufficient.

(E)   Statements (1) and (2) TOGETHER are NOT sufficient.

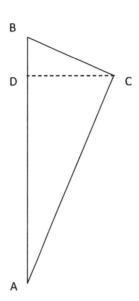

Note: Figure not drawn to scale.

BCA = 90°   DBC = DCA = 60°   AD = √3

61.   What is the area of the triangle ABC?

(A) $\dfrac{\sqrt{3}}{4}$

(B) $\dfrac{\sqrt{3}}{2}$

(C) $\dfrac{2}{\sqrt{3}}$

(D) $\sqrt{3}$

(E) $\dfrac{4}{\sqrt{3}}$

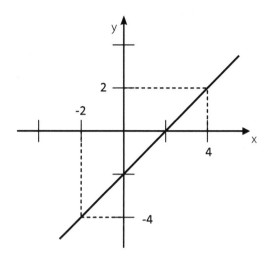

62.   What inequality includes all values of *x* where *y* < 0 for the line shown?

(A)   *x* < -4

(B)   *x* < -2

(C)   *x* < 0

(D)   *x* < 2

(E)   *x* < 4

63. What is the area inscribed by the lines $y = 1$, $x = 1$, $y = 6 - x$ on an xy-coordinate plane?

(A)   8

(B)   10

(C)   12

(D)   14

(E)   18

64.   A computer manufacturer claims that a perfectly square computer monitor has a diagonal size of 20 inches. However, part of the monitor is made up of a plastic frame surrounding the actual screen. The area of the screen is three times the size of that of the surrounding frame. What is the diagonal of the screen?

(A) $\sqrt{125}$

(B) $\dfrac{20}{3}$

(C) $\dfrac{20}{\sqrt{3}}$

(D) $\sqrt{150}$

(E) $\sqrt{300}$

65. A barn is enclosed in the shape of a 6-sided figure; all sides are the same length and all angles have the same measure. What is the area of the enclosed space?

(1) Each side is 100 feet long.

(2) The distance from the center of the barn to the midpoint of one of the sides is $50\sqrt{3}$ feet.

(A) Statement (1) ALONE is sufficient, but statement (2) alone is not sufficient.

(B) Statement (2) ALONE is sufficient, but statement (1) alone is not sufficient.

(C) BOTH statements TOGETHER are sufficient, but NEITHER statement ALONE is sufficient.

(D) EACH statement ALONE is sufficient.

(E) Statements (1) and (2) TOGETHER are NOT sufficient.

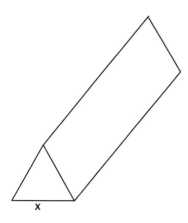

66. A chocolate box has a long triangular shape. The triangular shaped end piece is an equilateral triangle. The length of the box is $5\sqrt{3}$ inches, and the volume is 135. What is the value of x in inches?

(A) $\dfrac{9}{\sqrt{3}}$

(B)   3

(C)   6

(D)   9

(E) $9\sqrt{3}$

67. A small cubical aquarium has a depth of 1 foot. In the small aquarium there is a big fish with volume 44 cubic inches. A big cubical aquarium has depth of 2 feet and 88 fish, each with a volume of 2 cubic inches. What is the difference in the amount of water between the two aquariums if they are both completely filled?

(A)   246 cubic inches

(B)   300 cubic inches

(C)   11,964 cubic inches

(D)   13,824 cubic inches

(E)   16,348 cubic inches

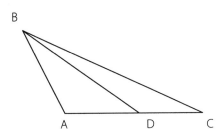

68.   In the figure above, D is a point on the side AC of △ABC. Is △ABC isosceles?

        (1)   The area of the triangular region ABD is equal to the area of triangular
                region DBC.

        (2)   BD ⊥ AC and AD = DC

(A)   Statement (1) ALONE is sufficient, but statement (2) alone is not sufficient.

(B)   Statement (2) ALONE is sufficient, but statement (1) alone is not sufficient.

(C)   BOTH statements TOGETHER are sufficient, but NEITHER statement ALONE
        is sufficient.

(D)   EACH statement ALONE is sufficient.

(E)   Statements (1) and (2) TOGETHER are NOT sufficient.

69. In an *xy*-coordinate plane, a line is defined by $y = kx + 1$. If $(4, b)$, $(a, 4)$, and $(a, b + 1)$ are three points on the line, where a and b are unknown, then $k = ?$

(A) $\frac{1}{2}$

(B) 1

(C) $1\frac{1}{2}$

(D) 2

(E) $2\frac{1}{2}$

70.   A cube has length x, a surface area y, and a volume z. Which of the following must be true?

(A) $\dfrac{xy}{z} - \dfrac{y}{x} = 0$

(B) $\dfrac{x^2y}{z} - \dfrac{y}{x} = 0$

(C) $\dfrac{xz}{x^2y} - \dfrac{x^2}{xy} = 0$

(D) $\dfrac{x\sqrt{y}}{\sqrt{z}} - \dfrac{x^2}{y} = 0$

(E) $\dfrac{\sqrt{z}}{xy} - \dfrac{\sqrt{y}}{x^2} = 0$

71.   A large cube is made up of smaller equally sized cubes, where each smaller cube has sides $\frac{1}{3}$ the length of the large cube. What approximate percent of the total volume is one of the small cubes?

(A)   3%

(B)   3.7%

(C)   9%

(D)   11.11%

(E)   33.33%

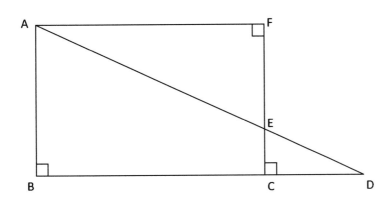

Note: Figure not drawn to scale.

72.   In the diagram above, BD = 8, AB = 6, and ED = 5. What is the area of ABCE?

(A)   16

(B)   18

(C)   20

(D)   22

(E)   24

73.   A glass is shaped like a right circular cylinder with a half sphere at the bottom.
       The glass is 7cm deep and has a diameter of 6cm, measured on the inside. If the
       glass is filled to the rim with apple cider, how much cider is in the glass?
       The formula for the volume a sphere is $\frac{4}{3}\pi r^3$.

(A) 18π

(B) 36π

(C) 54π

(D) 81π

(E) 108π

74.   Circle ABCD in the diagram below is defined by the equation $x^2 + y^2 = 25$. Line segment EF is defined by the equation $3y = 4x + 25$ and is tangent to circle ABCD at exactly one point. What is the point of tangency?

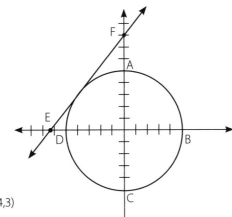

(A)   (-4,3)

(B)   (-3,4)

(C) $(-4, \frac{7}{2})$

(D) $(\frac{7}{2}, 3)$

(E)   (-4,4)

75.   A rectangular yard is 20 yards wide and 40 yards long. It is surrounded by a thick hedge that grows on the border of the property, but completely within the boundaries of the yard. If the hedge covers an area of 171 yards^2, what is the width of the hedge?

(A) $\dfrac{160}{120}$

(B) $\dfrac{171}{120}$

(C) $\dfrac{180}{120}$

(D) $\dfrac{191}{120}$

(E) $\dfrac{800}{120}$

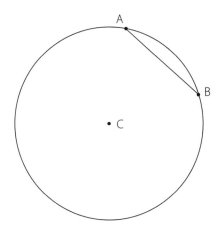

76.   In the attached figure, what is the area of the circle with center C?

        (1)   The length of minor arc AB is one sixth of the circumference.

        (2)   The length of chord AB is 8.

(A)   Statement (1) ALONE is sufficient, but statement (2) alone is not sufficient.

(B)   Statement (2) ALONE is sufficient, but statement (1) alone is not sufficient.

(C)   BOTH statements TOGETHER are sufficient, but NEITHER statement ALONE
        is sufficient.

(D)   EACH statement ALONE is sufficient.

(E)   Statements (1) and (2) TOGETHER are NOT sufficient.

77.   Line D passes through point (-2,5), and the product of its *x*-intercept and *y*-intercept is positive. Which of the following points could be on line D?

(A)   (5,10)

(B)   (-3,2)

(C)   (-1,7)

(D)   (-1,2)

(E)   (-3,1)

78.   Find the distance between points (21, -5) and (30, 7) in the coordinate
        geometry plane?

(A)   10

(B)   12

(C)   15

(D)   182

(E)   35

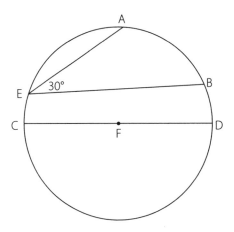

79.   What is the length of minor arc AB in the circle above which has a diameter of CD equaling12?

(A)   2π

(B)   4π

(C)   6π

(D)   8π

(E)   It cannot be determined with the information given.

Solutions

Coordinate Geometry Drill Solutions

1. *If a line has a positive slope which two quandrants must the line pass through? What if it has a negative slope? Give the equation for a line that passes through only quadrants I and II.* If a line has a positive slope, that line must always pass through quandrants I and III. If a line has a negative slope, that line must always pass through quandrants II and IV. The equation $y = 3$ (slope of 0) is an example of a line that passes through quandrants I and II only.

2. *Find the point where $y = 3x + 5$ and $y = -2x - 10$ intersect.* Remember, the point at which two linear equations intersect on the coordinate geometry plane is simply the solution for those two equations. In other words, at that one point, the values for x and y are the same in each equation, so we are allowed to subsitute and solve algebraically. In this case, $y = 3x + 5$ and $y = -2x - 10$, so $3x + 5 = -2x - 10$, $5x = 15$, and $x = -3$. If $x = -3$ then $y = -4$ and the point is (-3,-4).

3. *What are the equations for the y-axis and the x-axis?* The equation for the y-axis is $x = 0$ and the equation for the x-axis is $y = 0$.

4. *Arrange the following equations in ascending ordered based on the value for their x intercepts. Do the same for their y intercepts.*
A. $6 + 12x = 3$ B. $x + 2y = 8$ C. $15x + 5y + 10 = 0$

To find the x and y intercepts, we must first reorder the equations in the form $y = ax + b$

A. $y = 4x + 2$ B. $y = \frac{1}{2}x + 4$ C. $y = -3x - 2$

For the x intercepts, compare the values of $-\frac{b}{a}$ for each equation.

A. $-\frac{1}{2}$ B. $+8$ C. $\frac{-2}{3}$ In ascending order, it is C,A,B.

For the y intercepts, compare the values of b for each equation.

A. 2   B. 4   C. -2   In ascending order, it is C,A,B.

5. *What is the area of the triangle formed by the intersection of the lines $y = 2x - 2$, $y = -\frac{1}{2}$*

$x + 8$, and $y = 0$? To solve this problem you must find the x intercepts for the first two

equations and the point where those two equations intercept. The third boundary ($y = 0$)

is the x-axis. The x intercepts for the two equations are 1 and 16. The point at which they

intercept is (4,6). Therefore the height of the triangle is 6 and the base is 16 - 1 = 15. The

area is thus .5(6)(15) = 45. This is a more difficult problem.

Lesson Solutions

1. (B)

Since the two angles form a straight line, $x^2 + 3x = 180$. Subtract 180 from both sides to

get $x^2 + 3x - 180 = 0$. This factors to $(x + 15)(x - 12) = 0$. x must be 12, since an angle cannot

be -15 degrees (or any other negative number).

2. (A)

When you learn in Statement (1) that angle DEF is 96 degrees, you can be sure that it is

not one of the equal angles (because doubling it would be more than 180 degrees), so

the other two angles must each be 42 degrees. Therefore statement (1) is sufficient and

the answer is A or D. In the second statement, you are not sure whether Angle DEF is one

of the equal angles or whether it is the unequal angle, so it is impossible to make any

conclusions about the other angles. As a result, the answer is A.

3. **(C)**

First, simplify the root given in the original question. 243 is really $3 \cdot 81$ so it is possible to pull out the perfect square and use the simplified equivalent of $9\sqrt{3}$. Now, the equation for the area of an equilateral triangle can be applied by plugging in the area and solving for the side s: $9\sqrt{3} = \frac{s^2\sqrt{3}}{4}$. We then use basic algebra skills to solve for s and quickly find that it is equal to 6. The perimeter is therefore 3(6) or 18. The answer is C.

4. **(A)**

Since 7 and 10 are the lengths of two sides of a triangular region, the length of the third side, x, must be greater than $10 - 7$, or 3, and less than $7 + 10$, or 17. So, $3 < x < 17$. Thus, of the three lengths given, 2, 8, and 17, only 8 can be the length of the third side. Therefore, the answer is A.

5. **(B)**

Because DE is parallel to AC, angle BED must equal angle BCA and angle BDE must equal angle BAC. From this knowledge we know that triangles BDE and BAC are similar triangles. As a result we know that all corresponding sides are in the same proportion. In other words: $\frac{BD}{BA} = \frac{BE}{BC} = \frac{DE}{AC} = \frac{heightBDE}{heightBAC}$. Using this knowledge we know that the proportion is 5:10 because we are given the value of DE and AC. To determine the area of BDE we only need the height and we will be able to use the $\frac{1}{2}b \cdot h$ formula as we know the base (DE) = 5. Because the problem gives us the area of the larger triangle and its base, we can determine the height of the larger triangle. That height = 8 and it is determined by $A = \frac{1}{2}b \cdot h$ formula for the area of a triangle. Once we know the height of the larger triangle we can determine the height of the smaller triangle by using the proportion of the similar triangles. In other words $\frac{5}{10} = \frac{heightBDE}{8}$, so height BDE = 4 and the area of BDE $= \frac{1}{2}(5)(4) = 10$.

6. **(B)**

The area of a trapezoid is the average of the parallel sides multiplied by the height. With this knowledge, this is a very easy question – simply $6 \cdot 3 = 18$. However, if you do not know the formula, this is a question that will be impossible to answer.

7. **(B)**

Height is $\sqrt{100} - \sqrt{36} = 8$. Length of base is $\frac{360}{8} = 45$. Perimeter is $45 + 45 + 10 + 10 = 110$.

8. **(C)**

Statement (1) implies that Q is a rhombus that may or may not be a square. Therefore, the answer is B, C, or E. Statement (2) alone does not imply that Q is a square since any rectangle or isosceles trapezoid has diagonals of equal length. Therefore, the answer must be C or E. If (1) and (2) are considered together, Q is a rhombus that has diagonals of equal length. Since only a square has both properties, Q is a square and the answer is C.

9. **(A)**

$x + y = 180$ and $x - y = 100 \rightarrow x = 40$ and $y = 140$ and $z = 40$. Taking the measure of z and dividing by 360, we get $\frac{40}{360} = \frac{1}{9}$

10. **(B)**

We know that to solve this problem, we want to eventually find the internal angle of arc KL. Since the lines are parallel, we know that angle LMN must also be 25°. From the rule about the relationship between the angle from either the radius or diameter to a given point on a circle, we know that angle LON is twice the angle LMN, or 50°. Finally, we know KOM must also be 50° if the lines are parallel, leaving us with an internal angle KOL of 80°. Now we can solve for arc KL: $\frac{80}{360} \cdot \pi \cdot d = \frac{2}{9} \cdot 12\pi = \frac{8\pi}{3}$. See the diagram at the top of the opposite page.

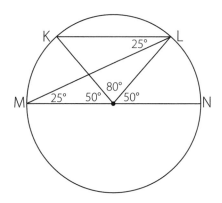

11. **(D)**

Questions that ask for the area of an undefined shape – that is, a shape other than a triangle, circle, or quadrilateral that you have studied – will always require you to find the difference between shapes for which you can find the area. In this case, you can quickly anticipate that the area of a circle will come in to play, and you will also need to recognize that the area of a triangle will be used. In this question, because we are told that the circles are identical and perfectly tangent to one another, we know that the radii of the circles will form an equilateral triangle with sides of twice the radius, or 12. Because the triangle is equilateral, we also know that all angles are 60 degrees:

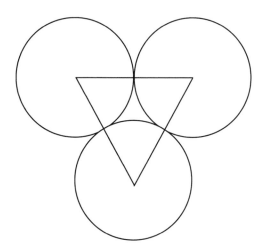

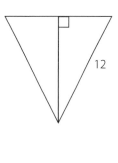

When taking the area of an equilateral triangle, the height will create two identical 30-60-90 triangles, allowing us to use that ratio to find its sides. Thus, with the hypotenuse already known as 12, the height will be $6\sqrt{3}$, and the area of the big triangle will be $\frac{1}{2}$ (12 · $6\sqrt{3}$) or $36\sqrt{3}$. To find the shaded area, we will start with the area of the triangle, and subtract the three partial circles to find the remaining area. Because we know that the angles are each equal to 60 degrees, each circular region will equal $\frac{60}{360}$ (or $\frac{1}{6}$) of the area of a circle. With each radius of 6, the area of each circle is 36π, $\frac{1}{6}$ of which is 6π. There are three identical regions to be subtracted, for a total of 3 · 6π, or 18π. Thus, the area of the shaded region is equal to the area of the triangle minus 18π, and the answer is $36\sqrt{3}$ - 18π.

12. **(E)**

For this problem it may be helpful to draw a diagram.

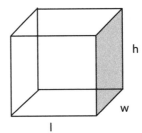

From statement (1) you only know that $h = 25$, but since you don't know l or w, (1) is not sufficient to solve for the volume of the tank and the answer must be B, C, or E. From statement (2), you know that $2(lw + wh + lh) = 3{,}300$, but since you don't know any of the dimensions, the answer must be C or E. From (1) and (2) together you know that $2(lw + 25w + 25l) = 3{,}300 \rightarrow (lw + 25w + 25l) = 1{,}650$, but you still need to know either the length of the width of the tank to determine its volume.

13. **(B)**

For this problem it may be helpful to draw a diagram.

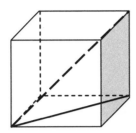

The volume of a cube is s^3, so each side must be 5 cm long. From this we can use the Pythagorean theorem or the properties of a 45-45-90 triangle to determine the diagonal of the bottom face of the cube to be $5\sqrt{2}$. Finally, we determine the length across the two farthest corners by again using Pythagorean theorem, now with the height of the cube and the diagonal of the base as the two sides. This gives us the following:

$\sqrt{5^2 + (5\sqrt{2})^2} = \sqrt{25 + 50} = \sqrt{75} = 5\sqrt{3}$.

14. **(B)**

Solve using the midpoint formula. The average of the x coordinates is $\frac{(3+5)}{2} = 4$. The average of the y coordinates is $\frac{(9-3)}{2} = 3$. Thus the midpoint is (4, 3). The answer is B.

Assorted Solutions

15. **(D)**

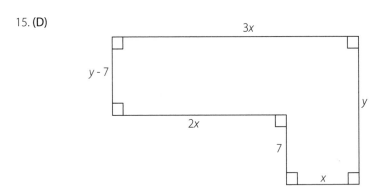

Since the figure is composed entirely of right angles, you know that the long side on top must equal the sum of the two sides parallel to it, $2x$ and x. Similarly, you know that the long side on the right, y, must equal the sum of the two sides parallel to it. Therefore the other missing side must equal $y - 7$. Add up all the sides to find the perimeter and set it equal to 50. Threrefore $3x + y + x + 7 + 2x + y - 7 = 50 \rightarrow 6x + 2y = 50$.

Solve for y: $2y = 50 - 6x \rightarrow y = 25 - 3x$.

16. **(E)**

Use the equation to find the x- and y-intercepts. If $x = 0$, then $y = 2$. Therefore point A is at (0,2). If $y = 0$, then $x = 4$. Therefore point B is at (4, 0). Thus AOB forms a right triangle with base 4 and height 2. Its area is $4 \cdot \frac{2}{2} = 4$. Follow the same process with I, II, and III to find the area of the triangle formed in each case. In case I, the x-intercept is at 4 and the y-intercept is at 1. Therefore the area is $4 \cdot \frac{1}{2} = 2$, which is half of 4. Case I works. In case II, the x-intercept is at 8 and the y-intercept is at 2, so the triangle formed is too big. In case III, the x-intercept is at 2 and the y-intercept is at 2, so the area of the triangle is $2 \cdot \frac{2}{2} = 2$. Case III works.

17. **(A)**

The outer circle has a radius of 12 inches. The inner circle is 11 inches. The area is equal to

$\pi(12^2 - 11^2) = \pi(144 - 121) = 23\pi$.

18. **(E)**

Original size $= 1 \cdot 1 \cdot 1 = 1$. New size $= 0.5 \cdot 0.5 \cdot 0.5 = 0.125$. $1 - 0.125 = .875$ or 87.5%.

19. **(B)**

We need to look at cross-sectional triangle that is perpendicular to the base and includes

the point at the top of the pyramid. This triangle has base 6 and height 10. We want half

of this. It is a right triangle with base 3 and height 10. Per the Pythagorean theorem, the

hypotenuse is $\sqrt{109}$. Now looking at the pyramid from one side, we have a triangle with

base 6 and height $\sqrt{109}$. The surface area, excluding the base, is the area of 4 equivalent

triangular faces $= 4 \cdot (\frac{1}{2}) \cdot 6 \cdot \sqrt{109}$.

20. **(E)**

Statement (1) alone is not sufficient to answer the question because R could have the

same dimensions as S (e.g., 4 : 2) and be silver, or R could have different dimensions

(e.g., 8 : 1) and not be silver. Thus the answer is B, C, or E. Statement (2) alone does not

tell anything about the relationship between the other sides of R and S, and so it is not

sufficient; the answer must be C or E. The logic applied to (1) can also be applied to the

information given in 2); thus (1) and (2) together are not sufficient, and the answer is E.

21. **(D):**

The circumference is π times diameter $= \pi d = 12\pi$, and half of it remains $= 6\pi$.

Since 4 diameters remain $= 4 \cdot 12 = 48$. The perimeter is $6\pi + 48$.

22. **(D)**

$8x + 4h = 480 \rightarrow h = 120 - 2x$

23. **(D)**

Answer	2x	12 side	15 side	Area	Height	Volume
A	10	2	5	10	5	50
B	8	4	7	28	4	112
C	6	6	9	54	3	162
D	**4**	**8**	**11**	**88**	**2**	**176**
E	2	10	13	130	1	130

24. **(A)**

The volume of a cylinder is the area of the circular base times the height:

Area $= \pi(r)^2 \cdot$ height $= 54\pi$

Since diameter $= 2r =$ height, then $r = \frac{1}{2}d = \frac{1}{2}h$.

Therefore, Area $= \pi\left(\frac{1}{2}\text{height}\right)^2 \cdot$ height $= 54\,\pi \rightarrow$ Area $= \pi\left(\frac{h^2}{4}\right) \cdot h = 54\pi \rightarrow$

Area $= \pi\left(\frac{h^3}{4}\right) = 54\pi \rightarrow$ Area $= \pi\frac{h^3}{4} = 54\pi \rightarrow h^3 = \frac{54\pi}{1} \cdot \frac{4}{\pi} \rightarrow h^3 = 216 \rightarrow h = 6 \rightarrow h = d = 6$

25. **(D)**

An excellent way to solve this problem is to plug in for y: use easy numbers such as $y = 4\pi$

gives us $r = 2$ and thus $d = 4$. Substituting $y = 4\pi$ into the answer choices shows us that

(D) is the correct answer. Algebraically, $A = y = \pi r^2$, thus $r = \sqrt{\frac{y}{\pi}}$ and $d = 2\sqrt{\frac{y}{\pi}}$.

26. **(D):**

Statement (1) gives us a right triangle with sides 3 and 4. Thus, the hypotenuse (which is

also the radius of the circle) is 5. This is sufficient to answer the question. Statement (2)

directly gives us the radius of the circle, so this is also sufficient to answer the question.

27. **(B)**

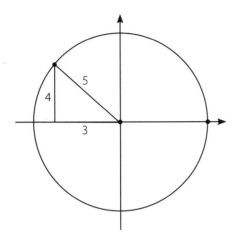

Since the figure is drawn to scale, the easiest way to solve this problem is to estimate the location of y given the x position of 4. Also, you could see that since the slope is constant, the slope determined from the two original points must be equal to the slope determined using either of the two original points and point E, but this way is more time-consuming ($m_1 = m_2 = \dfrac{(0 - 3)}{(6 - 0)} = \dfrac{(x - 3)}{(4 - 0)}$. Through either method, the y-coordinate of point E comes out to be 1.

28. **(A)**

The map below shows the consecutive paths that Fred rode in his roundabout trip from Town S to Town T.

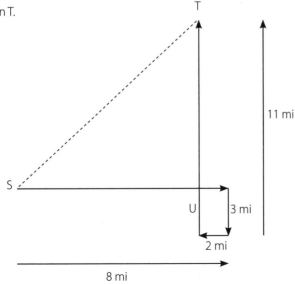

From the map, it be seen that his path crossed at point U and that SU = (8-2) or 6 miles and TU = (11 − 3) or 8 miles. Thus, by the Pythagorean Theorem, the straight line distance (dotted line) is $\sqrt{6^2 + 8^2}$ = 10 miles, and the answer is A.

29. (C)

Since the 6 pieces of wood are identical, each piece must have an area of 4 ft². Thus, the length of each piece is 2 ft long, and we can solve for the volume of the cube (which in turn is the amount of dirt the box can hold), or s^3, which comes out to be 8.

30. (D)

From (1), the diameter of the circle is equal to the side of the square, or 3 meters, and the area of the uncovered region is $9 - \pi(\frac{3}{2})^2$. Therefore, the answer must be A or D. From (2), the radius of the circle is $\sqrt{2.25}$ = 1.5 and the side of the square is 2(1.5) = 3. Therefore, the area of the uncovered region is $3^2 - 2.25\pi$.

31. (D)

There is no need to actually graph the lines to obtain the answer in this problem. The point that falls outside the region is the only point that does not satisfy the equation given above when the points are substituted into the equation. All of the points satisfy the equation except for (D).

32. (E)

If x is the length of a side of a square television screen and d is the length of the diagonal, then by the Pythagorean Theorem, $x^2 + x^2 = d^2$, $2x^2 = d^2$, and finally $x^2 = \frac{d^2}{2}$, which is the area of the screen in square inches. If $d = 19$, then the area $= \frac{192}{2} = \frac{361}{2}$ = 180.5 in². If $d = 21$, then the area $= \frac{212}{2} = \frac{441}{2}$ = 220.5 sq.in. Thus, the area of the 21-inch screen is greater by 220.5 − 180.5 = 40 square inches. Therefore, the answer is E.

33. **(B)**

An excellent way to solve this problem is to plug in numbers. If we select $a = 35$ we know that the angle LMN =105 because the angles in a triangle total 180. Thus, we can now see that $b = 40$. Plugging $a = 35$ into the answer choices, we find that (B) equals 40. This could also have been solved algebraically for the large triangle using the rule of 180.

34. **(B)**

Statement (1) implies that PQ=QR; however, the base PR may or may not equal PQ, and so (1) alone is not sufficient. Thus the answer must be B, C, or E. Statement (2) implies that PQ=QR, or that PQ is not greater than PR. Therefore, the answer is B.

35. **(E)**

Statement (1) is possible, but it is not a "must be true" statement. Imagine if L3 is the x-axis, then L1 and L2 would both be perpendicular to L3 if they were both parallel to the y-axis, but they would also both be perpendicular to L3 if L1 were parallel to the z-axis and L2 were parallel to the y-axis. The same logic shows that Statement (II) and Statement (III) are also not "must be true" statements.

36. **(C)**

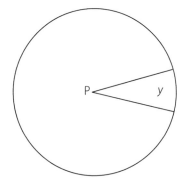

If P is the center of the circle above, then the fraction of the area of the circular region y is $\frac{y}{360}$. Since vertical angles are equal, the sum of the central angles of the two regions is $360 - 2(120)$, or 120. Therefore, $\frac{120}{360}$ of the circular region is marked with the letter y.

37. **(D)**

$\pi r^2 h \rightarrow \dfrac{(\pi r^2 h)}{4}$. Volume decreases to 25%. Price stays at 75%. Hence, price is three times the volume, or in other words, it has increased by 200%.

38. **(C)**

For this problem, drawing a figure may be helpful:

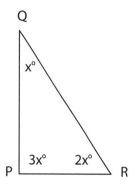

From statement 1, we can determine the proportion of the angles in the triangle as x, $2x$, and $3x$. Solving for x, noting that the sum of the angles must be equal to 180, we find that we are dealing with a 30-60-90 triangle. Given one length, we would be able to then determine the other two sides, but because such information is not given, statement 1 alone is insufficient, eliminating answer choices A and D. From statement 2, we are given the height, but do not have any other information regarding the triangle - angles, area, or other sides - that could help us determine the other sides. Thus, statement 2 alone is insufficient, eliminating answer choice B. Taking both statements together, we know from statement 1 that, in a 30-60-90 triangle, the sides will be of the proportion x, $\sqrt{3x}$, $2x$. Statement 2 gives us one of the sides, which then allows us to apply the proportions to find all sides, adding them together to find the perimeter. Thus, both statements taken together are sufficient to solve the problem, and the correct answer is C.

39. **(A)**

250π kg. First, the volume of the cylinder has to be calculated, in cubic feet, so it can be multiplied times the weight of the sand. The volume of a cylinder is the area of its base x height. If the diameter is 1, the radius is $\frac{1}{2}$ and the area of the circular base is $\frac{1}{4}\pi$ ft.² Since the height is 5 feet, the volume of the cylinder is $\left(\frac{\pi}{4} \text{ ft.}^2\right) \cdot 5 \text{ ft.} = \frac{5}{4}\pi$ ft.³

40. **(E)**

Statement (1) alone is not sufficient , because even though the figure could be a rectangle, it could also be a trapezoid. Statement (2) alone is also not sufficient, because while the figure could be a rectangle, it could also be another shape, such as a parallelogram. When Statements (1) and (2) are combined, we can see that angles *c* and *d* are each 90 degrees, but we still don't know the values for *a* or *b*. Still insufficient.

41. **(D)**

If the square's sides are 4 feet long, it's area is $4 \cdot 4 = 16$ inches² . Therefore, an equation can be formed for the area of the circle: Area = $\pi(r)^2$ (**take the square root of both sides**) $\rightarrow$ $\sqrt{16 \text{ inches}^2} = \sqrt{\pi(r)^2}$ (**simplify**) $\rightarrow$ 4 inches = $\pi(r)$ (**divide by π**) $\rightarrow \frac{4}{\pi} = r$.

42. **(B)**

This problem can be easily solved by plugging in the answer choices. One other way to solve it is to realize that, because the figure is a parallelogram, $5x + (2x + 5) = 180$, and thus we can solve for $x = 25$. Then we can use the rule of 180 for the triangle to get $x + 5x + 2y = 180$, and since we know $x = 25$, we can solve for $y = 15$.

43. **(C)**

This problem can be solved in a couple of different ways. One way is to realize that there are three different possibilities for the base of the box (which constrains the radius of the cylinder): $6 \cdot 12$, $6 \cdot 14$, or $12 \cdot 14$. In each case, the diameter of the cylinder will be determined by the smaller dimension. You can then solve for the resulting volume in the three situations and pick the one with the largest volume. An alternate approach would be to realize that the volume of a cylinder is $\pi \times r^2 \times h$, so since the radius is squared it has a greater role in the outcome than the height does. Thus, the maximum volume will most likely result when the radius is maximized, which occurs when the base of the cylinder is placed on the $12 \cdot 14$ face of the box. This means that the base of the cylinder is 36π, multiplied by the height of 6, which means that the volume of the cylinder is 216π.

44. **(C)**

Neither (1) nor (2), considered separately, gives sufficient information to answer the question since each provides information about only three of the six faces. Therefore, the answer must be C or E. From (1) and (2) together, it can be determined that $\frac{1}{4}$ of the surface area of the cube is red. The answer is C.

45. **(C)**

Since the area of the base is 9π, the radius must be 3. The greatest distance between two points is from one side of the base to the other, while moving the whole height of the cylinder. Draw the figure:

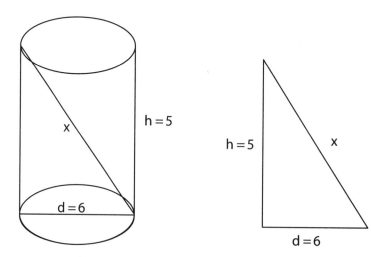

Use the Pythagorean Theorem to solve for x: $x = \sqrt{5^2 + 6^2} = \sqrt{25+36} = \sqrt{61}$.

46. **(B)**

The area of a circle is $A = \pi(r)^2$. If r doubles $\rightarrow 2r$.

Thus $A = \pi(2r)^2 = \pi(4r^2) = 4(\pi \cdot r^2) = 4A$

47. **(B)**

The formula for the area of a parallelogram is base $\times$ height, so we can get all the information needed from the point $(2, 3)$. All the other information provided is unnecessary. The point $(2, 3)$ tells us that the base is 2 and the height is 3. Thus, the area is $2 \cdot 3 = 6$.

48. **(D)**

One way to solve this problem is by assigning simple values for the two different sizes of pizza. If we say the radius of a medium pizza is 10, which gives us an area of 100π, then the radius of a large pizza must be 13, which has an area of 169π. Thus, the percent increase is $\frac{69\pi}{100\pi} = 69\%$.

49. **(B)**

If the length of RT is $5\sqrt{2}$, then it can be determined that altitude SU from S to side RT has length $5\sqrt{2}$, since $(\frac{1}{2})(5\sqrt{2})h = 25$. If this altitude coincides with side SR, then RST is a right triangle and, by the Pythagorean theorem, the length of the hypotenuse ST may be computed and the perimeter determined. However, side SR need not be perpendicular to side RT, in which case the perimeter cannot be determined. Therefore, (1) alone is not sufficient and the answer must be B, C, or E. From (2) alone, two sides of the triangle are equal and are perpendicular to each other. If these two sides have length x, then $(\frac{1}{2})x^2 = 25$ and $x = 5\sqrt{2}$. Now that the lengths of the legs are known, the hypotenuse can be determined using the Pythagorean theorem, and then the perimeter of the triangle can be computed. Therefore, (2) alone is sufficient, and the answer is B.

50. **(C)**

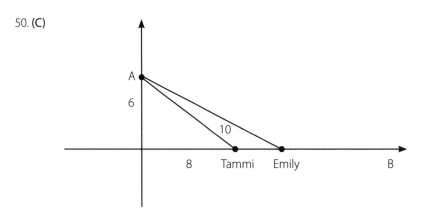

For Tammi, we know the total distance is 10, so the hypotenuse of a right triangle with another side of 6 is 10. Thus, by using the Pythagorean theorem or 6:8:10 triangle properties, we can find the other leg of the triangle to be 8. For Emily, the base of the right triangle is the 8 we just determined plus the 4 additional yards for Emily. Thus, she ran the length of the hypotenuse of a right triangle with two sides of 6 and 12, which gives us $6^2 + 12^2 = 180 = c^2$. Thus $c = \sqrt{180} = \sqrt{36 \cdot 5} = 6\sqrt{5}$. Finally, to find out how many more yards Emily ran, we subtract 10 from $6\sqrt{5}$, so the answer is $6\sqrt{5}$-10.

51. **(C)**

A figure should be drawn to more easily visualize the problem. We are essentially trying to find the area of a 120 degree segment of a circle with radius 9. Thus, the answer is $\frac{120}{360} \cdot \pi \cdot 9^2 = 27\pi$.

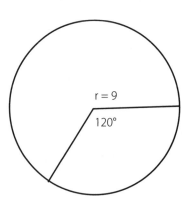

52. **(E)**

Since all the figures have the same angles and sides, and they are parallelograms, we just need to find the area of one of them and multiply that area by three. For each of the parallelograms, the area is the base times the height, so given that the sides are all equal to 4 and the angle is 60 degrees, we know the base is 4 and can solve for the height using the 30:60:90 triangle rule. The height ends up being $2\sqrt{3}$, and thus the area of one parallelogram is $8\sqrt{3}$. Finally we multiply by three to get the answer of $24\sqrt{3}$ for all the shaded figures.

53. **(E)**

The area of the triangular patio is found by the formula $A = \frac{1}{2}$(altitude)(base) or $30 = \frac{1}{2}(a)(a + 7)$. Thus, $a^2 + 7a = 60$. Factoring yields $(a + 12)(a - 5) = 0$, and $a = 5$ since the length must be positive. The base of the region is $5 + 7 = 12$, and the patio is a 5–12–13 triangle. The hypotenuse c can be found by using the Pythagorean theorem. Thus, the correct answer is E.

54. **(E)**

The volume of a right circular cylinder can be found by using the formula $V = \pi r^2 h$. If the size B container has radius r and height h, then the size A container has radius $3r$ and height $3h$. Thus, the volume of container A is $\pi(3r)^2(3h) = 27\pi r^2 h$, or 27 times that of the size B container. Since container A is only filled to half its capacity, it contains 13.5 times as much soup as container B, so the cost of the soup in container A is 13.5($2) = $27.

55. **(A)**

Since ZW = ZX = ZY, the interior triangles are all isosceles, and thus the other angles of △WXY have degree measurements as indicated in the figure on the next page. Since the measures of the three angles of a triangle always add up to 180°, it follows that:

$60 + (20 + r) + (40 + r) = 180$

$120 + 2r = 180$

$2r = 60$

$r = 30.$

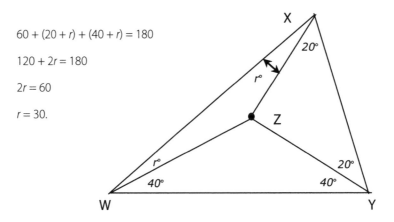

56. **(D)**

The area of the rectangle is length times width, or $x - 4$ times x. Form an equation relating the given information: $(x - 4)(x) = 252 \rightarrow x^2 - 4x = 252$ (**move everything to one side**) $\rightarrow$ $x^2 - 4x - 252 = 0$ (**factor**)$\rightarrow (x + 14)(x - 18) = 0$ (**solve for x**) $\rightarrow x = 14$ or $x = 18$. If $x = 14$, then $x - 4 = 10$. The area of the rectangle would thus be $10 \cdot 14 = 140$, not 252. As a result, this is wrong. If $x = 18$, then $x - 4 = 14$. The area of the rectangle would thus be $18 \cdot 14 = 252$. Therefore, this is the right answer, and D is the correct answer choice.

57. **(E)**

The equation of the x-axis is $y = 0$. The equation of the lines 2 units and 3 units to the right of the y-axis are $x = 2$ and $x = 3$, respectively. Thus, the answer cannot be A, B, or C. The top boundary line passes through the point $(1, 0)$. For the top boundary line to be correctly represented, at least two points on the line, say $(1,0)$ and $(2,1)$, must satisfy a given equation. The equation in answer choice E yields $0 + 2 = -\frac{1}{2}$ and $1 + 4 = -\frac{1}{2}$, respectively, which are both false. Thus, $y + 2x = -\frac{1}{2}$ is NOT an equation of one of the boundary lines, and the correct answer is E.

58. **(C)**

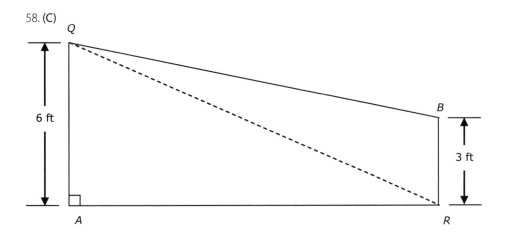

From the figure above, the area of the trapezoidal cross section is as follows:

$\frac{1}{2}$ (AQ + BR)(AR) $= \frac{1}{2}$ (3 + 6)(AR) $= \frac{9}{3}$ (AR). Since QR = 10 feet, using the Pythagorean theorem, AR $= \sqrt{(10^2 - 6^2)} = \sqrt{64} = 8$ feet. Thus, the area is $\frac{9}{2}(8) = 36$ feet.

59. **(D)**

Since the seating section is 10 feet wide, its outer boundary forms a circle with a radius $50 + 10 = 60$ feet. The area of the seating section can be found by finding the area of a circle with a radius of 60 feet and subtracting the area of a circle with a radius of 50 feet. The area of the seating section is therefore $\pi(60)^2 - \pi(50)^2 = (3,600 - 2,500)\pi = 1,100\pi$ square feet. Thus, the correct answer is D.

Challenge Solutions

60. (D)

Since angle XYZ is inscribed in a semicircle, it is a right angle, and XYZ is a right triangle. XYZ is divided into two right triangles by the vertical line from Y to side XZ. Let a = XY and b = YZ. The larger right triangle has hypotenuse b, so $b^2 = 16 + r^2$, and the smaller right triangle has hypotenuse a, so $a^2 = 16 + q^2$. From XYZ, $(q + r)^2 = b^2 + a^2$, so by substitution, $(q + r)^2 = (16 + r^2) + (16 + q^2)$. Therefore, $q^2 + 2qr + r^2 = 32 + q^2 + r^2$, and $qr = 16$. From statement (1), $q = 2$, so r must be 8, and the diameter YZ is 10, which means the length of the semicircle is P= $\frac{2\pi x5}{2}$ or 5π, from the equation P = $2\pi r$. (Note: you do not have to solve for the length of the semicircle, you just have to know that you can derive the value of the length by knowing the diameter of the semicircle). Thus, statement (1) alone is sufficient. From statement (2), $r = 8$, so q must be 2, and statement (2) alone is sufficient. Thus, EACH statement ALONE is sufficient to answer the question. The correct answer is D.

61. (C)

From the given information, it can be determined that DBC, DCA, and ABC are all 30-60-90 triangles with its specific properties. With this knowledge, or with the Pythagorean Theorem, it can be calculated that DC = 1 and CA = 2. Since AC = 2, and it is opposite a 60° angle, BC, which is opposite a 30° angle, is $\frac{2}{\sqrt{3}}$. As a result, AB, the side opposite the 90° angle, is twice that, or $\frac{4}{\sqrt{3}}$. The area of a triangle is one half · base · height. In this case, that is equal to AC · BC = $\frac{1}{2} \cdot 2 \cdot \frac{2}{\sqrt{3}} = \frac{2}{\sqrt{3}}$.

62. (D)

Look at the graph on the next page. Since the y-axis is the vertical axis, the horizontal hatches that intersect with the y-axis correspond to values of y, e.g. 2 and -4 are values of y. It must be determined where the line intersects $y = 0$, since the question refers to all points $y < 0$. $y = 0$ at $x = 2$, as shown with the point on the opposite page:

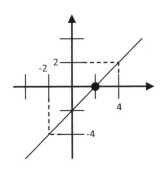

The slope of the line is such that all values of y correspond to x values less than 2 (to the left of the dot). Therefore, answer choice D is the correct response.

63. **(A)**

Draw the picture to help visualize the area. (Draw the line $y = 6 - x$ by knowing that the y-intercept is 6, and the slope is -1 and intersects the x-axis at $x = 6$.) The area of a triangle is $\frac{1}{2}$ base $\cdot$ height. The base of this triangle extends from $x = 1$ to $x = 5$; thus, the base is $5 - 1 = 4$. The height of this triangle extends from $y = 1$ to $y = 5$; thus, the height of this triangle is $5 - 1 = 4$.

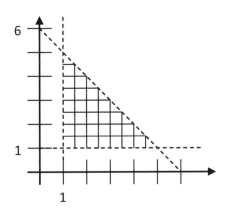

$\frac{1}{2}(4 \times 4) = 8$. Therefore, the answer is A.

64. **(E)**

The area of the entire monitor is side^2. Since the monitor's diagonal divides the square into a 45-45-90 triangle, a diagonal of 20 has a base of $\frac{20}{\sqrt{2}} = 20\left(\frac{1}{\sqrt{2}}\right) = 20\left(\frac{\sqrt{2}}{2}\right) = 10\sqrt{2}$. The

Pythagorean theorem can also be used: side^2 = $(10\sqrt{2})^2$ = 200 = area of entire monitor. Since the area of the screen is 3 times the size of the frame, the frame, x, plus the screen, 3x, equals the total area of the monitor: $x + 3x = 200 \rightarrow 4x = 200 \rightarrow x = 50$. Therefore, the area of the screen is $3x = 3(50) = 150$. Since side^2 is the area of the screen, the following equation can be used to find a side of the screen: side^2 = 150 $\rightarrow$ side = $\sqrt{150}$. The side of a 45-45-90 triangle times $\sqrt{2}$ is the length of the diagonal: $\sqrt{150} \cdot \sqrt{2} = \sqrt{300}$ is the length of the diagonal. Thus, answer choice E is the correct response.

65. **(D)**

For this problem, drawing a figure may be helpful:

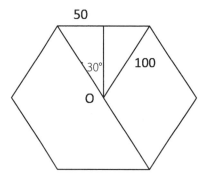

Since all six sides have the same length and the six interior angles have the same measure, the barn encloses a space equal to six triangles of the same size. Since there are 360 degrees around the central point O, each of these triangles has a 60° angle at point O. The other two angles of each triangle are equal and so must also be 60°. Therefore the six triangles are equilateral triangles and the area of the enclosed space is 6 times the area of any of these triangular regions. From statement (1) you can determine that the altitude OP shown in the figure has length 50$\sqrt{3}$ feet and that the area of the enclosed space is $(50\sqrt{3})(50)(6)$ square feet. Therefore, the answer must be A or D. Similarly, from statement (2) you can determine that the length of each side is 100 feet, and thus the total area is 15,000$\sqrt{3}$ square feet.

66. **(C)**

The volume of the long triangular shape should be derived from the volume of a cylinder. The area of the triangular base times the length should equal the volume of the triangular shape, as in the following equation:

$$\text{area of a triangle} = \frac{\text{volume}}{\text{length}} = \frac{135}{5\sqrt{3}} = \frac{27}{\sqrt{3}} = \frac{27}{\sqrt{3}}\left(\frac{\sqrt{3}}{\sqrt{3}}\right) = 9\sqrt{3}$$

Dividing an equilateral triangle in half results in a 30-60-90 triangle, as shown below: Thus, the height can be calculated as shown, and the area of the triangle is as follows:

$$\frac{1}{2}\left(\frac{\sqrt{3}}{2}x^2\right) = 9\sqrt{3} \rightarrow \frac{\sqrt{3}}{4}x^2 = 9\sqrt{3} \rightarrow x^2 = 36 \rightarrow x = 6$$

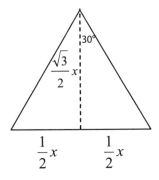

67. **(C)**

Since the small aquarium is cubical and one foot deep, it is $(12 \cdot 12 \cdot 12)$ inches^3 =1728 inches^3. The large aquarium possesses a depth of 2 feet, or 24 inches, and is thus $(24 \cdot 24 \cdot 24) = 13,824$ inches^3. The fish in the small aquarium has a volume of 44 cubic inches, so there are $1,728 - 44 = 1,684$ cubic inches of water. The fish in the large aquarium fill $88 \cdot 2 = 176$ cubic inches, so there are $13,824 - 176 = 13,648$ cubic inches of water. The difference between the two = $13,648 - 1,684 = 11,964$ cubic inches.

68. **(B)**

From the fact in (1) that the area of region ABD is equal to the area of region DBC, and the fact that the two triangles have the same altitude from B, it can be determined that AD = CD, but not that △ABC is isosceles. Thus, (1) alone is not sufficient, and the answer must be B, C, or E. From (2) it follows that $\triangle ABD$ and $\triangle DBC$ are right triangles. Since

$AD = CD$ and BD is a common side, it follows, by the Pythagorean theorem, that $AB = BC$,

and so $\triangle ABC$ is isosceles. Thus (2) alone is sufficient, and the answer is B.

69. (A)

Plug in the coordinates:

$y = kx + 1$

$(4, b) : b = 4k + 1$

$(a, 4): 4 = ak + 1$

$(a, b + 1): b + 1 = ak + 1$

Use the equations to solve for the value of k. Since $ak + 1 = 4$ and

$ak + 1 = b + 1 \rightarrow ak + 1 = b + 1 = 4$

From this equation, b can be solved for: $b + 1 = 4 \rightarrow b = 3$

Since $b = 4k + 1$ and $b = 3$, $3 = 4k + 1 \rightarrow 2k = 4 \rightarrow k = \frac{1}{2}$.

70. (B)

In one dimension, only length exists. In two dimensions, length and width exist, resulting

in a product of surface area. In three dimensions, length, width, and height exist, resulting

in volume. With a cube, length, width, and height are all of equal length. Therefore,

$length^2 = $ surface area of a single side, and $length^3 = $ volume, or $6x^2 = y$, $x^3 = z$, $x\left(\frac{y}{6}\right) = z$

and $\frac{6z}{y} = x$. Now analyze the answer choices by putting all variables in terms of x. Only

answer choice B equals 0: $\frac{x^2 y}{z} - \frac{y}{x} = \frac{x^2 (6x^2)}{x^3} - \frac{6x^2}{x} = 0$.

71. (B)

Since the volume of a cube equals side $\cdot$ side $\cdot$ side, or $side^3$, when the sides change, the

volume changes by an even greater amount. Let x represent the length of a side, where

the volume of the larger cube is equal to x^3. If x becomes $\frac{1}{3}x$, then the volume of the

smaller cube is $\dfrac{\frac{1}{27}x^3}{x^3} = \dfrac{1}{27}$ of 100%, or $\dfrac{100}{27}$ %. Of the answer choices, answer choice A is

closer to $\dfrac{100}{33\frac{1}{3}}$. Answer choices C, D, and E are way too large. $\dfrac{100}{27}$ is closest to 3.7; therefore,

answer choice B is the correct response.

72. (B)

This is a bit of a tricky problem since the figure is somewhat distorted compared to what

the numbers indicate it actually looks like. As alternate angles, angle AEF must equal angle

CED. Pythagorean theorem shows that AD = $\sqrt{AB^2 + AD^2} = \sqrt{6^2 + 8^2} = \sqrt{100} = 10$. we know

ED = 5 so AE = AD – ED = 10 – 5 = 5. Since all the angles in triangle AEF are equal to those

in triangle CED, and since these triangles have the same length hypotenuse, these two

triangles are identical. Thus, EF = EC, and EF + EC= 6, so EF = 3. Using Pythagoras again we

find that AF = 4. So the square ABCF has area = 6 · 4 = 24. And the triangle AEF has

area = 0.5 · 4 · 3 = 6, and the area ABCE = 24 - 6 = 18. Therefore the answer is B.

Solution 2:   Given the right angle at B, the area of triangle ABD is $(\frac{1}{2})$*6*8 = 24 Given the

right angle at B and the lengths of line segments AB and BD, triangle ABD is a 6 - 8 - 10 (3 -

4 - 5) right triangle. Given that ECD is a right angle and the angle at D is shared by triangle

ADB and triangle EDC, triangles ADB and EDC are similar triangles. Since EDC is similar to

ADB and we know ED is 5, CD and EC must be 4 and 3, respectively. The area of triangle

EDC is $(\frac{1}{2})$ * 4 * 3 = 6 The area of space ABCE is the area of triangle ABD less the area of

triangle EDC = 24 - 6 = 18, so answer choice (B) is correct.

73. (C)

Volume of half sphere = $\dfrac{2\pi(3)^3}{3} = 18\,\pi$

Volume of cylinder = $\pi\,3^2(7-3) = 36\,\pi$

Total volume = 54π

74. (A)

This is a difficult geometry problem (if you do not backsolve) that requires some seemingly tedious algebra (it works out quite well in the end). Importantly, students must understand that at the point of tangency, x and y are solutions for each equation. In other words, it is possible to solve simultaneously for $x^2 + y^2 = 25$ and $3y = 4x + 25$ to find the one point of tangency. To do that, solve for y in the second equation and then substitute in the first: $y = \frac{4}{3}x + \frac{25}{3}$. Then substituting in the first equation for the circle, you see that $x^2 + \left(\frac{4}{3}x + \frac{25}{3} \right)^2 = 25$. Using your knowledge of the common algebraic equation $(x + y)^2$ you can quickly expand the parantheses to make the equation look like this:

$x^2 + \frac{16}{9}x^2 + \frac{200}{9}x + \frac{625}{9} = 25$. Simplify this equation by mulitplying both sides by 9 to remove all fractions: $9x^2 + 16x^2 + 200x + 625 = 225$.

Combine like terms to get the equation in the form of a quadratic: $25x^2 + 200x + 400 = 0$. Divide through by 25 to get: $x^2 + 8x + 16 = 0$. This is an easily factored quadratic as it is a perfect square: $(x + 4)^2 = 0$ and $x = -4$ so $y = 3$. The answer is (-4,3).

> *Lazy Genius:* After recognizing that the point of tangency must be a solution for both equations, use the answer choices. The values of x and y in that point must solve both equations and only answer choice A does that.

75. **(C)**

Subtracting the area of the hedge (171 yds² from the overall area (20 · 40 = 800 yds²), we can determine that the area of the yard not covered by the hedge is 629 yds². If we assign the variable "x" to the width of the hedge, the inner area can also be expressed as $(20 - 2x)(40 - 2x) = 629$. Since solving for this equation will likely require the quadratic equation, it is likely best to glance at the answer choices to determine if back solving for x will be a quicker way to answer this question. Because the answer choices A and C easily factor in to manageable fractions ($\frac{4}{3}$ and $\frac{3}{2}$, respectively), back solving looks like a much less painful and time consuming way to attack this problem from here. Quickly looking at the possibilities for back solving, an astute test-taker will notice that using answer choice C, the reduced fraction $\frac{3}{2}$ will factor easily with the $2x$ term, so it is likely easiest to begin with choice C. Using $\frac{3}{2}$ as the first trial, the equation becomes: $629 = (20 - 2 \cdot \frac{3}{2})(40 - 2 \cdot \frac{3}{2}) = (20 - 3)(40 - 3) = 17 \cdot 37$. $17 \cdot 37$ does equal 629, and thus the problem is solved using answer choice C.

Note that, given the time-consuming nature of multiplying multiple-digit numbers, the back solving technique can best be applied by quickly multiplying the ones digits to determine if the corresponding ones digit of the product matches with the necessary answer (629). Because, in the case of answer choice C, 7 · 7 does produce a ones digit of 9, it becomes necessary to multiply the entire product. If it did not produce a 9, one could quickly determine that the product would be unequal to 629, and thus move on to the next answer choice.

76. **(C)**

With the first statement, it is possible to determine the measure of central angle ACB with your knowledge of arcs and central angles (60 degrees), but nothing else. With the second statement, you learn the length of chord AB but that does not help you determine the area of the circle by itself. Therefore, each statement alone is not sufficient. Together it is possible to determine the radius and thus the area, because triangle ABC is isosceles. Remember that all radii are equal so AC = CB and consequently angle CAB equals angle CBA. Because the third angle is known from statement (1) (60 degrees), you can determine that the remaining 120 degrees is split evenly between CAB and CBA, and all angles are 60 degrees. As a result, triangle ABC must be equilateral and all sides are 8. With that knowledge, you can determine the area of the circle which is 64π. Answer is C.

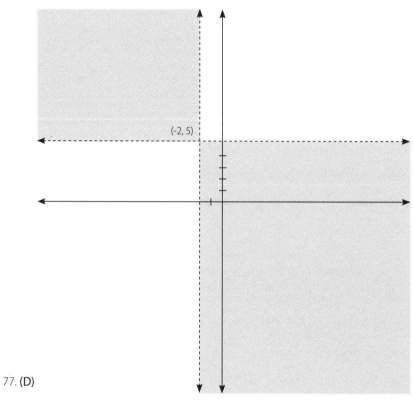

(-2, 5)

77. (D)

For the product of the intercepts to be positive, they must both be positive or both be negative. Looking at the accompanying diagram, you can see the area where such a point could fall so that the line has either both positive or both negative intercepts. This is a qualitative coordinate geometry question, which is common on the actual GMAT. Do not try to write out equations for each set of points; simply use your understanding of the coordinate geometry plane to pick the one point that meets the conditions given in the problem. Answer is D as shown in the diagram.

78. (C)

To answer this you can either use the distance formula: The distance between any two points (x_1, y_1) and $(x_2, y_2) = \sqrt{(x_1 - x_2)^2 + (y_1 - y_2)^2}$ and do the calculations to see that $\sqrt{(30 - 21)^2 + (7 - (-5))^2} = \sqrt{9^2 + 12^2} = \sqrt{225} = 15$ OR simply reason the answer out with your knowledge of the Pythagorean Thereom. In any distance problem such as this, you

are looking for the hypotenuse of a right triangle whose legs are the difference between the respective *x* and *y* coordinates. Here you know the two legs are 9 and 12, so with your knowledge of common right triangles (this is a multiple of a 3,4,5 triangle) you know the answer is 15.

79. **(A)**

To solve for minor arc AB, you must first determine the circumference of the circle. If the diameter is 12, then the radius is 6 and the circumference is $2\pi r = 12\pi$ (or simply πd). Remembering your rules for inscribed angles, you know that there is a relationship between inscribed angle AEB, which is cutting out minor arc AB, and central angle AFB (not shown in the diagram), which cuts out the same arc. If angle AEB is 30 degrees then the central angle must be twice that or 60 degrees. If the central angle is 60 degrees, then the arc represents $\frac{1}{6}$th of the circumference or 2π. Answer is A.

Answer Key

Lesson

1 . . . . . . B
2 . . . . . . A
3 C
4 . . . . . . A
5 . . . . . . B
6 . . . . . . B
7 . . . . . . B
8 C
9 . . . . . . A
10 . . . . . B
11 . . . . . D
12 . . . . . E
13 . . . . . B
14 . . . . . B

Assorted

15 . . . . . . D
16 . . . . . . E
17 . . . . . . A
18 . . . . . . E
19 . . . . . . B
20 . . . . . . E
21 . . . . . . D
22 . . . . . . D
23 . . . . . . D
24 . . . . . . A
25 . . . . . . D
26 . . . . . . D
27 . . . . . . B
28 . . . . . . A
29 C
30 . . . . . . D
31 . . . . . . D
32 . . . . . . E
33 . . . . . . B
34 . . . . . . B
35 . . . . . . E
36 C
37 . . . . . . D
38 C
39 . . . . . . A
40 . . . . . . E
41 . . . . . . D
42 . . . . . . B
43 C
44 C

45 C
46 . . . . . . B
47 . . . . . . B
48 . . . . . . D
49 . . . . . . B
50 C
51 C
52 . . . . . . E
53 . . . . . . E
54 . . . . . . E
55 . . . . . . A
56 . . . . . . D
57 . . . . . E
58 C
59 . . . . . . D

Challenge

60 . . . . . . D
61 C
62 . . . . . . D
63 . . . . . A
64 . . . . . E
65 . . . . . . D
66 C
67 C
68 . . . . . . B
69 . . . . . A
70 . . . . . . B
71 . . . . . B
72 . . . . . . B
73 C
74 . . . . . A
75 C
76 C
77 . . . . . . D
78 C
79 . . . . . . A

THE MBA TOUR
Your future begins here

The MBA Tour offers Quality Interaction With Top Business Schools

MEET with school representatives at our OPEN FAIR

LISTEN to top school experts discuss valuable MBA admission topics at our PANEL PRESENTATIONS

DISCUSS individual school qualities with representatives at our ROUNDTABLE EVENTS

ASIA	UNITED STATES	SOUTH AMERICA	CANADA
TOKYO	HOUSTON	BUENOS AIRES	CALGARY
SEOUL	CHICAGO	SANTIAGO	VANCOUVER
TAIPEI	ATLANTA	SAO PAULO	TORONTO
BEIJING	NEW YORK	LIMA	MONTREAL
SHANGHAI	BOSTON	BOGOTA	
BANGKOK	WASHINGTON DC	MEXICO CITY	
SINGAPORE	LOS ANGELES		
	SAN FRANCISCO	EUROPE	
INDIA		MUNICH	
BANGALORE		LONDON	
NEW DELHI		PARIS	
MUMBAI			

Register at www.thembatour.com

THE MBA TOUR
Your future begins here